Southern Living

Sheds
& Garages

Oxmoor House®

Southern Living® Sheds & Garages **was adapted from a book by the same title published by Sunset Books.**

Consulting Editors: Don Vandervort, Giles Miller-Mead, Jane Horn.
Editorial Coordinator: Vicki Weathers

Senior Editors: Jim McRae, Pierre Home-Douglas
Assistant Editor: Jennifer Ormston
Writers: Stacey Berman, Adam van Sertima
Art Directors: Philippe Arnoldi, Odette Sévigny
Picture Editor: Sonia Di Maulo

Special Contributors: Gilles Beauchemin, Eric Beaulieu, Linda Cournoyer, Lorraine Doré, Martin Francoeur, Dominique Gagné, Sara Grynspan, Christine Jacobs, Rob Lutes, Jacques Perrault, Maryo Proulx, Mathieu Raymond-Beaubien, Jean Sirois, Judy Yelon.

Cover Design: Vasken Guiragossian
Photography: Van Chaplin

Our appreciation to the staff of *Southern Living* magazine for their contributions to this book.

First printing January 1999
Copyright © 1999 by Oxmoor House, Inc.
Book Division of Southern Progress Corporation
P.O. Box 2463, Birmingham, Alabama 35201
All rights reserved, including the right of reproduction in whole or in part in any form.

Southern Living® is a federally registered trademark of Southern Living, Inc.

ISBN 0-376-09065-0
Library of Congress Catalog Card Number: 98-87050
Printed in the United States

Acknowledgments
Thanks to the following:
APA-The Engineered Wood Association, Tacoma, WA
Martin Berman, Laval, Que.
Serge Caron, Howick, Que.
The Chamberlain Group, Inc., Elmhurst, IL
The Chittenden Bank, Burlington, VT
Clopay Building Products Company, Cincinnati, OH
Richard Day, Palomar Mountain, CA
Garage Door Services, Fontana, CA
National Association of Home Builders, Washington, D.C.
PCS Automation Services Inc., London, Ont.
Peinture Sico, Outremont, Que.
Sears, Roebuck and Co., Hoffman Estates, IL
The Shed Shop, Fremont, CA
Shelter-Kit Incorporated, Tilton, NH
Society of American Registered Architects, Lombard, IL
Southern Forest Products Association (Southern Pine Council), Kenner, LA
Stanley Door Systems, Troy, MI
Gisèle Thibault, St. Urbain Premier, Que.

Picture Credits
p. 4 Hampton/Crandall
p. 5 *(upper)* Van Chaplin
p. 5 *(lower)* Jean Allsopp
p. 6 *(upper)* Sylvia Martin
p. 6 *(lower)* Colleen Duffley
p. 7 *(upper)* Crandall & Crandall
p. 7 *(lower)* Mike Dobel/Masterfile
p. 8 *(upper)* Robert Perron
p. 8 *(lower)* Sonia Di Maulo
p. 9 *(upper)* Sonia Di Maulo
p. 9 *(lower)* Robert Perron
p. 10 *(upper)* Janice Boudreau
p. 10 *(lower)* Crandall & Crandall
p. 11 *(upper)* Grant/Crandall
p. 11 *(lower)* Sylvia Martin
p. 12 *(upper)* Crandall & Crandall
p. 12 *(lower)* Emily Minton
p. 13 *(upper)* courtesy Southern Forest Products Association
p. 13 *(lower)* Crandall & Crandall
p. 14 *(upper)* Van Chaplin
p. 14 *(lower left)* courtesy Paul Johnston/The Shed Shop
p. 14 *(lower right)* Van Chaplin/photo styling: Sybil Sylvester
p. 15 Breyer/Crandall

Design Credits
p. 5 *(upper)* Architect (front door surround): Steve Goggans. Landscape architect: Robert C. Chesnut
p. 5 *(lower)* Architects: Bill Curtis and Russell Windham, Curtis & Windham Architects
p. 6 *(upper)* Architect: Bob Johnson, Johnson & Rosser, Architects
p. 6 *(lower)* Architects: J. Carson Looney, AIA (Principal in Charge); Bradford K. Shapiro, AIA (Project Architect), Looney Ricks Kiss Architects, Inc. Builder: Ben H. Reisman, Prestige Development, Inc. Interior designer: Steve Bengel, Bengel Designs. Landscaping: Sheldon Reynolds Company, Inc.
p. 11 *(lower)* Landscape architect: Eddie Browder, Hugh Dargan Associates
p. 12 *(lower)* Architect: Joey Horne

CONTENTS

A GALLERY OF GARAGES AND SHEDS

For many people in the past, garages and sheds were almost an afterthought—something quickly erected when the house was finished, with only a quick nod to design and utility. No more. Today's homeowner can choose from a variety of styles to suit any purpose and to complement any home design.

Still, many of the reasons for building a garage or a shed remain unchanged, from storing tools to parking the family car. But both structures can still be as attractive as they are practical—a pleasure to look at and to use. Style of roof, number of doors, choice of siding: Each of these elements can be adapted to suit your home and your landscape.

As the photos on the following pages show, the designs of garages and sheds—and the purposes they fulfill—can be as varied as a home itself. The only limitation is your budget. And your imagination.

A little bit of effort on the exterior can make a big difference to the appearance of a shed. Here, latticework provides a convenient way to add some greenery to dress up a backyard structure.

GARAGES

The roof style and siding of the garage shown above match those of the house, leading the eye from one structure to the other without any jarring distractions.

Although spacious, this garage with second-story studio doesn't overpower its site. Careful design and detailing turn a big, square box into a lively little backyard cottage. (Cars enter from a drive-way, to the right.)

A garage can serve as a focal point as well as a practical shelter for cars. With its steeply pitched roof, cedar-shingle siding, and gently arched doorways, this one recalls a romantic barn or covered bridge.

A standard two-car garage would dominate this narrow lot. Extending the entry porch creates a single-width carport that recalls the wraparound porches of the past.

Instead of one large door, the two-car garage shown above has two doors that nicely divide the front of the structure into symmetrical halves.

Sometimes the smallest things make the biggest difference. Here, a cupola atop the garage adds the perfect crowning touch.

By orienting the doors of the attached garage at 90° to the house—instead of parallel to it—the designers of this structure chose to create a seamless view of the two buildings when seen from the front.

A blend of two styles: The long, sloping roof of the garage at right, with its pronounced overhang in the front, gives the structure a shed-like look.

*One advantage of a
gambrel roof, especially
for a two-story garage,
is that it provides plenty
of headroom on its
second floor—space
which would otherwise
be lost with a steeply
pitched roof.*

*Archways in front of the
garage below frame
the structure's two doors.
The triangular arch over
the entry door to the
house is reflected in the
garage dormer, adding
more symmetry.*

Different needs give rise to different sheds: This utilitarian structure is used exclusively to store the firewood that will keep a stove stoked for a long Vermont winter.

The builders of this shed borrowed from a traditional Cape Cod saltbox design. A shake roof adds to the rustic charm and complements the overall look of the building.

With its carefully finished siding and attractive window box, this shed looks—at first glance—like part of a house. In fact, it serves as a convenient storage place for sporting goods and equipment.

Tucked in a backyard, this storage shed was once a modest box of a building. Rather than hiding the structure, it was dressed up with rafters, columns, lattice, and a path paved with coastal sand shell.

The shed shown above, framed by plants on top and surrounding vegetation, looks like an outgrowth of the deck on which it was built, rather than a mere addition.

More than just a convenient place to stash the lawn mower, this simple potting shed also anchors a corner of the property and frames the approach to a recently landscaped rear garden.

Although sheds come in an almost infinite variety of shapes and sizes, many still resemble the simple timeless design of the model shown at right, which served as the basis of the shed anatomy on page 22.

With its steep-pitched shake roof, arched doors, and decorative trim, this shed would prove an attractive addition to almost any backyard.

Rather than building a shed from scratch, you can buy one prefabricated. The structure below arrived quite plain, but paint, simple surface trim, and a new roof made from salvaged rusted tin gave it charm.

No matter how small your space, there is always room for a shed. Tucked in nicely under the eaves of a house, this one still offers plenty of storage. Check local codes if you are building near the property line.

Properly built and looked after, a shed will last almost indefinitely. An 1850s privy-turned-toolshed from a Louisiana plantation adds its weathered character to this garden, as well as providing needed storage.

Who says a shed has to look like a shed? This open and spacious model looks more like a gazebo than a typical backyard outbuilding. It features a Plexiglas roof and is designed principally to store gardening equipment.

PLANNING YOUR STRUCTURE

Garages and sheds may appear to be simple structures but their construction should not be taken lightly. Modern garages—and to a lesser extent, sheds—are constructed using many of the same fundamental techniques found in house construction: foundation work, carpentry, plumbing, wiring, and roofing, to name a few. And as with building a house, a good amount of planning is required before the construction of a garage or shed even begins.

This chapter will give you a few tips on planning your structure, beginning with evaluating your needs *(opposite)*. You'll find an anatomy of a typical garage, along with an overview of the key steps in its building sequence, beginning on page 19; turn to page 22 for the same sort of information on a shed.

Running the plumbing's feed and drain lines, which is especially important before laying the slab in a garage, is addressed on page 23, followed by details for wiring on page 24. Some of the important legal considerations to keep in mind when planning a new structure are listed on page 25.

Whether you hire a general contractor to do most of the work, or a tradesman to do one specific task, you'll first want to read the helpful information on working with professionals on page 26. And finally, if you plan on doing all or just some of the work yourself, turn to page 28 for a list of tools and safety equipment.

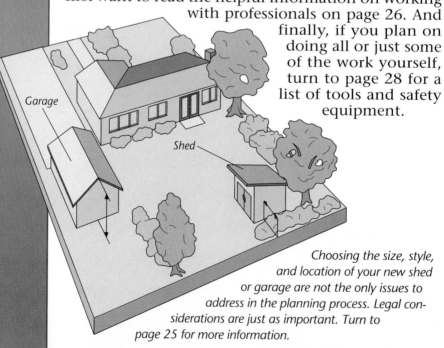

Garage

Shed

Choosing the size, style, and location of your new shed or garage are not the only issues to address in the planning process. Legal considerations are just as important. Turn to page 25 for more information.

EVALUATING YOUR NEEDS

The best way to evaluate your needs when deciding on the type of shed or garage to build is to focus on the purpose of the new structure. Will your shed simply be an answer to a storage problem, or will it double as workshop? Do you want a garage for the sole purpose of parking the car, or is added living space above an important option? Of course, needs vary from situation to situation, but deciding on the function of the new building is a good starting point in the planning process.

Any questions regarding the functionality of a new shed or garage are directly related to the size of the structure. For a shed, you'll want to make it large enough to comfortably store a lawn mower and garden tools, for example. A garage should have enough space for a car with room left over for bicycles and storage. (Minimum space requirements for single- and double-car parking are illustrated below and at right.) Apart from measuring the items you intend to store and allotting the necessary space in your plan, it's best to check with your building department before construction. Local restrictions may determine the structure's overall size, as well as its location on your property.

Apart from the size of the building you should also take into account ease of access and human traffic patterns. Generally, a garage should be near the house; sheds are more likely to be off in a corner (right, bottom). Also, make sure the driveway (page 18) doesn't divide a play or leisure area; children or guests shouldn't need to crisscross the drive when enjoying outdoor activities. And remember to consider the view. A poor choice can cause your prospective garage to obscure the best view from your house.

Unless existing elements such as trees and established flower beds and shrubs can be incorporated into the landscaping plan—shade trees are good to have near a workshop, for example—they may need to be removed to make way for the new structure. This is not necessarily a bad thing however, as a new

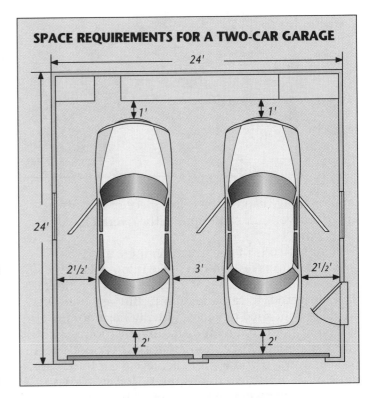

SPACE REQUIREMENTS FOR A TWO-CAR GARAGE

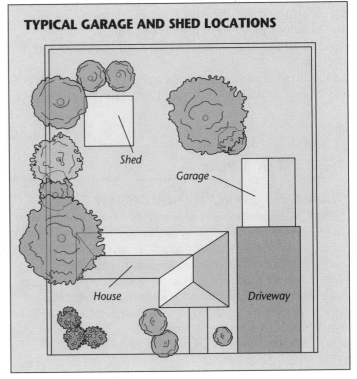

TYPICAL GARAGE AND SHED LOCATIONS

SPACE REQUIREMENTS FOR A SINGLE-CAR GARAGE

TWO TYPES OF DRIVEWAY LAYOUT

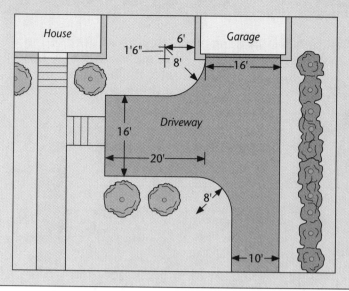

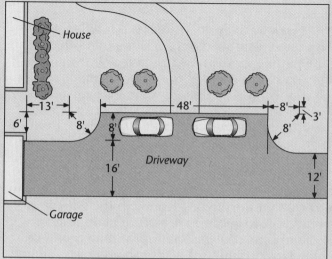

shed or garage can be the centerpiece of a landscaping makeover that can improve the overall look of your property

As for the style of the structure, there are two approaches to take: You can make it look like an extension of your home, or you can choose a different style altogether to call attention to the new building. To make your shed or garage visually harmonious with your home, plan on matching the roofing and siding materials. Also, choose the same type of doors and windows. If you want to achieve a contrast, vary some or all of the exterior features. However, try to maintain consistency in the design of the new building. For example, if you finish a shed in Victorian style, don't choose modern windows or contemporary-looking aluminum doors; details should not look out of place.

Of course, a new garage often requires a new driveway. Apart from the traditional straight design *(page*

17), driveways can include additional off-street parking or a turnaround area *(above)*. In most cases, longer driveways work best at a single car width, widening as necessary to access each door on the garage. Short driveways are more likely to be two car widths wide. Driveways that turn must be wider in order to accommodate the car's turning radius. It's also necessary to provide for a crown (a higher, rounded center) in your driveway to help shed moisture to either side. In snowy areas, limit its slope to a shallow incline so it will be easier to negotiate. Local ordinances can govern the specifications of the drive, so consult your building department for specific requirements and restrictions.

Adding a paved path to your shed is a good idea, as it helps prevent ruts forming in your lawn, if you make frequent trips with wheelbarrows, mowers, or the like. Another useful addition for a shed is a ramp, to aid egress with wheeled or heavy equipment.

 ASK A PRO

HOW CAN I FINANCE MY NEW GARAGE?

There are three main ways of financing your new garage: You can extend your mortgage, borrowing from the equity you have in your home; you can apply for a home equity loan, usually obtained at another institution than the one where you obtained your mortgage; or, you can apply for a personal loan. Generally, extending your mortgage offers the lowest rate of interest, but you should shop around at different institutions and compare the costs of the various loans. The Federal Housing Administration helps underwrite loans to home owners.

Your lending institution will want to know your income, your credit history, and your debt load. They may also want to see a copy of the plans. Providing the bank with an appraisal of your home's value is required when seeking an extended mortgage or home equity loan. However, the potential value of the new structure can be considered part of your home's value. This can increase the size of the potential loan, but you will have to sign an agreement specifying that the loan will only go toward the new structure.

GARAGE CONSTRUCTION

The size of a garage normally means that it requires a building permit, and is expected to conform to the applicable building code. As a result, its structure and construction are much the same as for a house. Both are often structured as platform frame buildings. An overview of the construction sequence starts on the following page.

The "platform" in platform frame construction consists of the foundation and the floor structure; in the case of a garage, these are often one and the same in the form of a concrete slab *(page 33)*. The walls are built up starting from the slab or subfloor. The frame is completed with ceiling and roof framing members. The walls, ceiling, and roof are composed almost entirely of 2-by dimension lumber, fastened together by nails, sometimes supplemented by metal framing connectors.

Over this frame, sheathing—usually plywood—provides a base for nailing on the exterior siding. At the same time, sheathing reinforces the frame. Many types of sheathing can eliminate the need for bracing in the frame; one exception is insulating foam sheathing, which adds no structural support. A layer of building paper or housewrap, sandwiched between the sheathing and siding, provides additional draft and moisture protection.

The roof has a deck of plywood fastened to the rafters; over this surface, roofing felt provides moisture protection. Roofing material, such as asphalt shingles laid in overlapping strips, completes the waterproof membrane. Drip edges help shed water and protect the eaves.

Doors and windows are installed before siding to ensure a seamless fit. Casings are then fitted over the siding and the window and door frames. Siding may consist of solid boards or sheet materials, as well as wood shingles, metal, and aluminum. Trim, fascia, and soffits at the eaves complete the exterior.

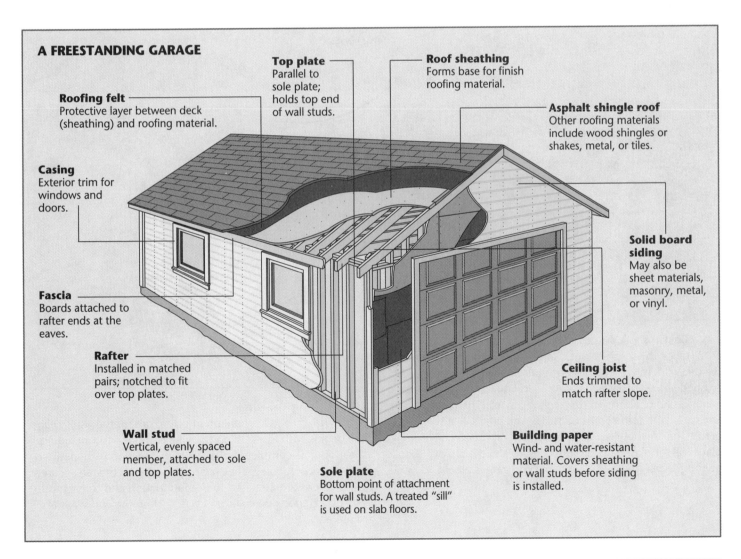

A FREESTANDING GARAGE

Roofing felt
Protective layer between deck (sheathing) and roofing material.

Top plate
Parallel to sole plate; holds top end of wall studs.

Roof sheathing
Forms base for finish roofing material.

Asphalt shingle roof
Other roofing materials include wood shingles or shakes, metal, or tiles.

Casing
Exterior trim for windows and doors.

Solid board siding
May also be sheet materials, masonry, metal, or vinyl.

Fascia
Boards attached to rafter ends at the eaves.

Rafter
Installed in matched pairs; notched to fit over top plates.

Ceiling joist
Ends trimmed to match rafter slope.

Wall stud
Vertical, evenly spaced member, attached to sole and top plates.

Sole plate
Bottom point of attachment for wall studs. A treated "sill" is used on slab floors.

Building paper
Wind- and water-resistant material. Covers sheathing or wall studs before siding is installed.

THE BUILDING SEQUENCE

There is a definite sequence to building a garage or shed. First, you must lay out the location of the foundation, according to your plans. The next stage is casting the foundation with concrete; plumbing should be roughed in, and inspected before concrete is placed. Once the concrete has cured, the walls are assembled and raised on the foundation. On top of the walls, rafters provide a frame, over which you lay sheathing, and the roof's outer surface, commonly asphalt shingles. Windows and doors are added, then siding is installed to finish the exterior walls. At this point, you can add utilities, and interior walls and ceilings if you wish.

Sheds require slightly different treatments, mostly because of their different foundations *(page 22)*. The steps are followed in the same order as shown on these two pages.

1 ▶ **Laying out the structure**
Before laying out the perimeter of your structure, check the drainage of your location and make any changes necessary to direct moisture away from the site *(page 31)*. Then use batterboards and mason's line to establish 90° corners using the 3-4-5 rule: Sides of 3, 4, and 5 feet—or any multiple of these numbers—will indicate that a corner is a right angle *(right)*. Once all the corners and sides are laid out with string, measure and mark the precise dimensions of the building.

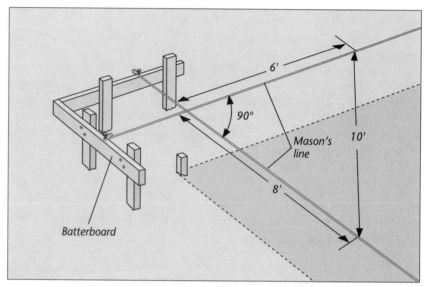

Batterboard · *Mason's line* · 90° · 6' · 8' · 10'

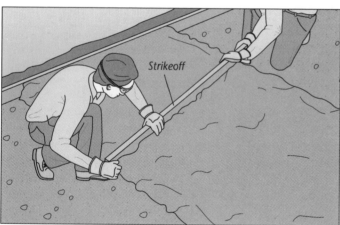

Strikeoff

2 **Casting the foundation**
Once the string layout is in place, you can dig the foundation. Its depth will depend on your area; you'll need to add crushed stone for drainage. Your foundation may consist of a floating slab or a footing sunk below the frostline *(page 33)*. In any case, your forms must be sturdy and precisely assembled, before the concrete is placed and struck off *(above)*. If your plans call for plumbing, all supply pipes and drain pipes should be roughed in *(page 23)* before the concrete is placed.

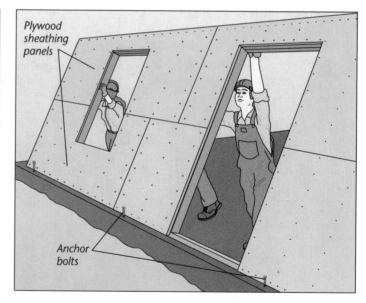

Plywood sheathing panels · *Anchor bolts*

3 **Raising the walls**
With a solid foundation in place, raising the walls *(page 45)* begins with assembling the wall components, including sheathing, as complete units. Each wall section is then raised into position *(above)*, checked for plumb and braced securely. The sections are attached to the foundation and to each other. The exterior side walls go up first, then the end walls are raised and "tied in."

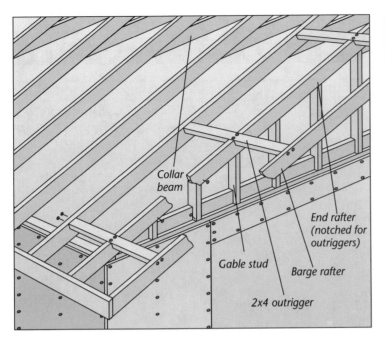

Collar beam

End rafter (notched for outriggers)

Gable stud

Barge rafter

2x4 outrigger

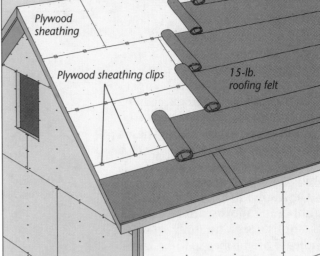

Plywood sheathing

Plywood sheathing clips

15-lb. roofing felt

4 Framing the roof

With the walls fixed in place, the roof, often a variation on the basic gable roof, can be assembled *(page 52)*. Either buy prefabricated trusses, or install rafters and ceiling joists or collar beams. Measure, assemble, and cut the rafters to fit over the top plate. The ridgeboard is fixed between the tops of the rafters, at the peak of the roof. Finish the job with gable studs, and barge rafters *(above)*.

5 Finishing the exterior

The first step in installing the exterior skin is adding the layers of roof decking, roofing felt, and shingles; this ensures some weather protection for the interior of the structure *(page 60)*. Next, doors and windows are installed *(page 64)*. The siding *(page 68)* goes on after, butted up against the doors and windows. Finally, trim, soffits, and fascias complete the structure, along with exterior door and window casings.

6 Finishing the interior

Most garages require wiring *(page 88)*; some may also need plumbing *(page 87)*. Both should be installed before you begin erecting the finished walls. Add insulation, if desired, and then cover the walls—gypsum wallboard *(left)* is a popular, inexpensive choice *(page 93)*. Interior trim can be as elaborate as necessary *(page 96)*. The concrete floor of a typical garage is best finished with a heat-resistant epoxy-based paint.

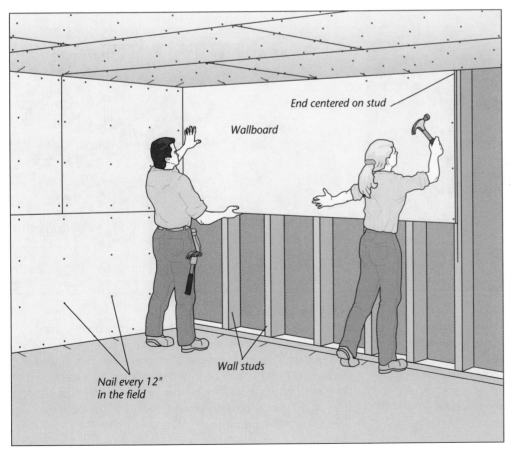

End centered on stud

Wallboard

Wall studs

Nail every 12" in the field

SHED CONSTRUCTION

Building your own shed is much like building a garage. The main difference is that most sheds are smaller, and aren't required to withstand the stresses of a larger structure. If your shed exceeds 100 square feet, it may be subject to building code regulations. These will indicate such requirements as the spacing and sizes of joists, studs, rafters, and beams.

Generally, the floor of a shed is composed of joists similar to those of a house. Structural plywood will indicate the proper span on the material itself: $5/8$-inch plywood, for example, can go over joists spaced 16 inches apart; $3/4$ inch is needed for 24-inch spans. Plywood rated 2-4-1, which is $1 1/8$ inches thick, allows the use of wider joist spans; it can serve as both a subfloor and a structural floor.

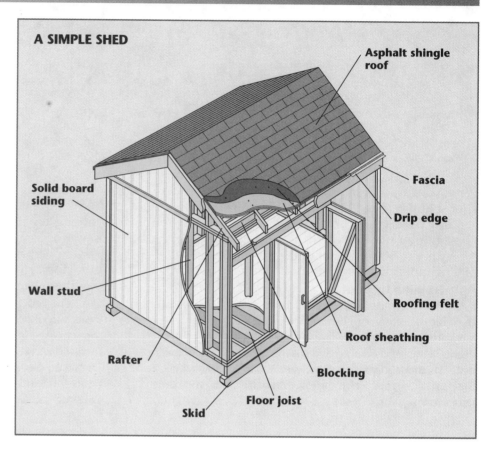

A SIMPLE SHED

Asphalt shingle roof

Fascia

Drip edge

Roofing felt

Roof sheathing

Blocking

Floor joist

Skid

Rafter

Wall stud

Solid board siding

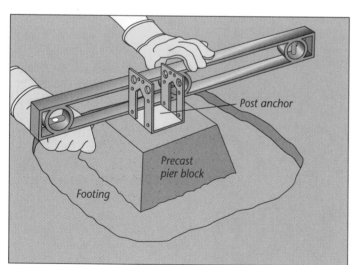

Post anchor

Precast pier block

Footing

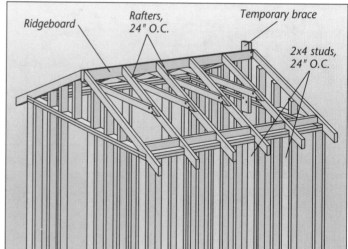

Ridgeboard

Rafters, 24" O.C.

Temporary brace

2x4 studs, 24" O.C.

Casting the piers
The simplest method for building concrete foundations is to cast a footing and set a precast concrete pier block on top of it *(above)*. The beam that supports the shed's floor joists rests in the post anchor on top of the pier. (In some cases, the beam itself will rest on top of a short post in the post anchor.) Alternatively, the shed can be built on wooden 6x6 skids *(page 40)*.

Framing the shed's roof
A shed requires much the same structure as any other framed building, but the rafters, joists, and studs can be spaced on 24-inch centers. The lighter stresses allow the use of 2x4s instead of the sturdier framing members used in garages. The exception is floor joists, which should not be smaller than 2x6s; in some cases, 2x8s or 2x10s may be necessary depending on the loads the shed's floor will support.

PLANNING FOR PLUMBING

When plotting out any plumbing addition there are a variety of considerations, including code restrictions, the limitations of your system's layouts, design, and, of course, your own plumbing abilities. Extending supply and drain-waste and vent (DWV) pipes to a new garage or shed requires the ability to measure pipe runs accurately, calculate DWV slope, and cut and join pipe and fittings; consider hiring a professional to check your plans and install the DWV system.

Don't buy a pipe, a fitting, or a fixture until you've checked your local plumbing and building codes. Almost any work will require approval from local building department officials before you start, and inspection of the work before you close the walls and floor. Learn what work you may do yourself—some codes require that certain jobs be done only by licensed plumbers.

Appropriate plumbing amenities will depend on the purpose of your structure. A basic garage or potting shed will be more useful with a simple hose bibb, but if you intend your shed as, say, a small painting studio, a full sink may be necessary. When planning your plumbing, keep in mind that while it's relatively easy to route supply pipes, it's more difficult to put in and conceal drainage and venting pipes. As a result, installing a hose bibb in your garage or shed is much easier than fitting a sink, with its hot and cold water, and the associated DWV system.

Your local plumbing code may specify exactly what type of pipe is appropriate for a given application. The cold water main, which provides your home's water, is typically 3/4- or 1-inch copper pipe. This branches into 1/2-inch pipes that serve all cold water fixtures; a separate pipe feeds the hot water heater, which branches in turn into 1/2-inch hot water pipes, made typically of copper, polybutylene plastic (PB) or galvanized iron. PB tubing and copper are common choices for do-it-yourselfers; copper may last longer, but PB is much easier to work with.

The DWV system uses PVC (polyvinyl chloride) or ABS (acrylonitrile-butadiene-styrene) plastic pipes to carry away wastes, and vent gas. PVC is a better choice than ABS because it is less susceptible to mechanical and chemical damage, and has a slightly greater variety of available fittings. The measurement of pipe refers to its outside diameter (O.D.).

Before you can add the new pipes, you'll need to pinpoint where they'll run in walls and floors, and where they'll tie in to the existing system. The water pipe should tap off the main house line that comes from the water meter, or utility shutoff valve, which is usually located at your property line. The DWV pipe must go out to the main sewer, joining it from above

with a Y fitting at a 45° or 90° angle. It's best if the DWV is below the frost line, but it's more important that it meets the sewer from above.

DWV systems rely on gravity to move wastes from the fixture to the sewer or septic tank. For this reason, drain outlets must be higher than the drain pipe. The ideal drain pipe slope is 1/4 inch down per foot. If the drain is too steep, water will drain too fast, leaving solids behind. The illustration below shows the position of the drain pipe before the slab is poured. The pipe extends high enough above grade so it's not covered when the slab is placed. And it extends straight down to below the frost line before turning to meet the sewer or septic tank.

In warm climates the installation and maintenance of plumbing can be easier; for example, in warm areas like southern California, you can bring the water pipe just barely below ground, and raise it outside the garage for a hose bibb. In colder climates, pipes should be buried below the frost line, and should come up through the slab; also, you'll need to heat the building to keep the pipes from freezing. A freeze-proof faucet can help protect your pipes from the cold, especially where they protrude through the exterior wall. Freeze-proof faucets are designed so the water retreats back into the pipes when the faucet is not in use. A larger piece of ABS pipe should surround the water pipe where it comes up through the slab. This prevents the pipe being broken should any frost heave occur. DWV pipe can be wrapped with an asphalt shingle, or some other sleeve, so it too can move within the slab.

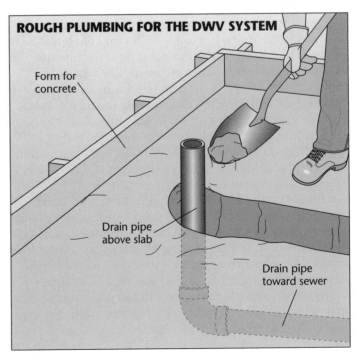

ROUGH PLUMBING FOR THE DWV SYSTEM

Form for concrete

Drain pipe above slab

Drain pipe toward sewer

PLANNING FOR WIRING

From powering electric lawn mowers to garage door openers, electricity is vital to many functions in a typical garage. Even in a shed, a simple light can make all the difference in the world. Fortunately for the do-it-yourselfer, electrical work is neat and logical. But before you embark on any wiring projects, such as adding a circuit to your garage or shed, it's important to understand a few things about electricity itself, electrical safety, and electrical codes.

You should start by evaluating your existing electrical system, and determining your needs for the new structure. If you just want lights and a couple of outlets, a single additional circuit may be all you require. But if your garage is to double as a workshop, or if you intend on powering numerous electrical appliances, you may require a sub-panel, supplying several new circuits.

It would be a time-consuming task to calculate your electrical usage by adding up the wattages of all your lights and appliances. However, after considerable research, the National Electrical Code (NEC) has established certain values that represent typical electrical use. The formula for calculating your estimated electrical needs is based on the amps per square foot of a given structure. The actual calculation is quite complex; refer to the NEC, or discuss your plans with an electrician.

Your service, provided by your local electrical utility, gives you a maximum amount of power; in a new home this will be at least 100 amps. If you're already consuming most of the power your service provides, you'll require a service panel with more amps, which must be installed by a licensed electrician or your electrical utility. This is expensive, so make sure you actually need it.

If your present service is sufficiently underutilized, and you need only a single 15- or 20-amp circuit, it is possible to run that circuit underground from your home's main service panel; either use UF-type cable, which can be buried directly in the ground at a minimum depth of 12 inches, or run cable through conduit. Rigid nonmetallic conduit (PVC schedule 40) is the best choice; it doesn't corrode, but requires a separate grounding wire. Rigid metallic conduit will eventually corrode and disintegrate in certain types of soil, but usually doesn't require a separate grounding wire. Grounding provides a path for electricity, so short circuits and water are less of a threat; a GFCI (ground fault circuit interrupter) receptacle provides additional, necessary protection. If you're laying UF cable, lay a redwood board on top before covering it with soil, to reduce the danger of spading through the cable at a later time.

Once the wiring is completed, remember to get it inspected before it is hidden by interior walls, floors, and ceilings.

LAYING OUT YOUR ELECTRICAL CIRCUIT

The first step in planning a new circuit is to draw a diagram showing the location of each proposed switch, receptacle, light fixture, and major appliance. The symbols in the legend below will make this easier. The next step is to design the circuit.

Keep in mind that you may want to have at least two circuits supplying the lights to your structure.

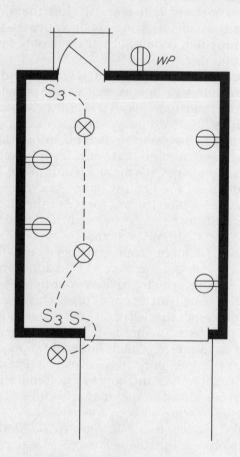

ELECTRICAL SYMBOLS

⊗   Light fixture

⊖   Duplex receptacle

S   Single-pole switch

S₃   Three-way switch

⊖ WP   Weatherproof receptacle

LEGAL CONSIDERATIONS

Before you've gone too far in planning your garage or shed, consult your local building department for any legal restrictions. In most areas, you'll need to file for a building permit and comply with building code requirements. Also be aware of local zoning ordinances, which normally govern such restrictions as easements and building height *(see illustration below)*.

Building permits: Before you pound a single nail, get the needed permits. It is important that the local building department check your plans to ensure you don't get off to a substandard start. Negligence may come back to haunt you: Officials can fine you, force you to bring your structure up to standard or have you dismantle it entirely. Since it is the contractor who must assume responsibility for following building code requirements, it is best to have the plumbing and electrical services installed by licensed professionals. They can obtain the permit, making them responsible for meeting the building code requirements. If you're doing all the work yourself, discuss your ideas with the building inspector and ask whether you'll need a permit. Sheds, for example, often require a building permit only when they exceed 100 square feet in size.

Fees are usually charged for permits based on the projected value of the new structure. Give an accurate estimate to avoid being overcharged.

Building codes: These codes vary from region to region. They set minimum safety standards for materials and techniques, such as depth of footings, size of beams, and proper fastening methods. The building code ensures the safety of the building for you, your family, and any future owner.

Zoning ordinances: These municipal restrictions limit the height of residential buildings, limit lot coverage (the proportion of a lot a building and other structures can occupy), specify setbacks (how close to the property lines you can build), and—in some areas—stipulate architectural design standards.

Variances: If the zoning department rejects your plan, you can apply for a variance at your city or county planning department. It's your task to prove to a hearing officer or zoning board of appeal that following the zoning requirements precisely would create "undue hardship," and that the structure you want to build will not negatively affect your neighbors or the community. If you plead your case convincingly, you may be allowed to build.

Architectural review boards: Neighborhoods with tight controls may require that your structure meet certain architectural standards—and that means submitting your plans to an architectural review board. Going through this process can dramatically increase the time required to get your project moving.

Deeds: Your property deed may also restrict your project's design, construction, or location. Review the deed carefully, checking for easements, architectural standard restrictions, and other limitations.

On-site inspections: Once you've had your plan approved, you must stick to it exactly. It is a good idea to have a building inspector check periodically during construction, rather than completing the structure and having it judged illegal.

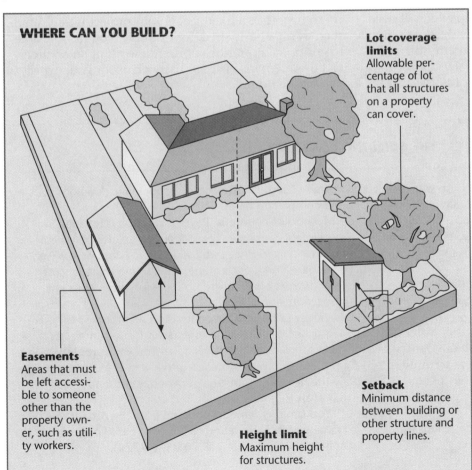

WHERE CAN YOU BUILD?

Lot coverage limits
Allowable percentage of lot that all structures on a property can cover.

Easements
Areas that must be left accessible to someone other than the property owner, such as utility workers.

Height limit
Maximum height for structures.

Setback
Minimum distance between building or other structure and property lines.

GETTING THE JOB DONE

The effort that you can contribute to any home building project depends on your knowledge, your abilities, your patience, and your health. Some jobs you can do yourself; for others, you may require some professional help. For example, you may prefer to do only the nonspecialized work, such as clearing the site for construction and cleaning up afterward, but hire experts for everything else. Or you may may decide to tackle all the work yourself. In any case, you need to consider the pros and cons.

WORKING WITH PROFESSIONALS

If you decide to consult a professional, be as precise as possible about what you want. Collect pertinent photographs from magazines, manufacturers' brochures, and advertisements. Describe the type of roofing and siding and any doors or windows that you want to use, and where you want to put them. If you have questions, write them down before the interview. It's a good idea to choose a professional who belongs to a trade association, because membership indicates a willingness to comply with the code of ethics adopted by the association. Also, if you do have a complaint, there is an established body that you can turn to with the problem.

Choosing an architect or designer: If you have decided to have custom plans drawn up, you will need to consult an architect or designer. Architects can draw up plans acceptable to building department officials. Some will also send out bids, help you select a contractor, specify materials for the contractor to order, and supervise the contractor's performance to ensure that your plans and time schedule are being followed. Designers (or design-build contractors, as they are often called) provide both design and construction services; they see your project through to completion, from drawing up the plans to the finishing details.

Licensing requirements vary from state to state. Some states that do require architects to be licensed do not require the same of design-build contractors; many design-build contractors don't charge for time spent in an exploratory interview. For plans, you'll probably be charged on an hourly basis. If you want an architect to select the contractor and keep an eye on construction, or if you hire a design-build contractor for the project, try to negotiate a fixed fee. If your project is very small, such as for a basic shed, for example, you may be able to entice an apprentice or drafter working in an architect or designer's office to draw plans for you; expect to pay by the hour.

THE BUILDING CONTRACT

A building contract binds and protects both you and your contractor. You can minimize the possibility of misunderstandings later by writing down every possible detail. (If you're acting as your own contractor, agreements with subcontractors should be put into writing.) The contract should include all of the following:

• **The project and participants:** Include a general description of the project, its address, and the names and addresses of both you and the builder.

• **Construction materials:** Identify grade of materials, quality of fasteners and, in the case of lumber, species. Indicate brand and model number of any accessories, such as lighting systems. Avoid the clause "or equal" that will allow the builder to substitute materials for your choices.

• **Work to be performed:** Specify all major jobs from grading to finishing.

• **Time schedule:** The contract should include both start and completion dates.

• **Method of payment:** Payments are usually made in installments as phases of work are completed. It is wiser to insist on a fixed price bid, though some contractors want a fee based on a percentage of labor and material costs. Final payment is withheld until the job receives its final inspection and all liens are cleared.

• **Waiver of liens:** If subcontractors are not paid for materials or services delivered to your home, in some states they can place a "mechanic's lien" on your property, tying up the title. Protect yourself with a waiver of liens, signed by the general contractor, subcontractors, and major materials suppliers.

You can buy a model contract from the American Homeowners Foundation (6776 Little Falls Road, Arlington, VA, 22213, Tel. 703-536-7776).

You may also choose to go with a ready-made plan for a design that suits your needs and taste. Starting on page 102 in this book is a section on plans that range from a simple shed to a three-car garage with living quarters.

Choosing a contractor: Licensed general contractors specialize in construction, although some have design skills and experience as well. Hired to build a small project, they may do all the work themselves; on a large project they assume responsibility for hiring qualified subcontractors, ordering construction materials, and seeing that the job is completed according to contract.

When you're looking for a contractor, it's best to ask architects, designers, and friends for recommendations. Meet with several contractors to discuss your project, and then call back only those whom you feel most comfortable with. To compare bids for the actual construction, give each contractor you are considering either an exact description of the job, complete with sketches, or the plans and specifications prepared by a professional. Be sure to include a detailed account of who will be responsible for what work.

Ask each contractor for the names and phone number of customers who've had projects similar to yours. Call several of these references, and discuss their level of satisfaction with the contractor; be sure to ask specific questions about whether the work was done on schedule, whether the site was well maintained, and whether they would hire the same contractor again; if you can, inspect the contractor's work. You can also contact the Better Business Bureau to find out whether there are existing complaints about the contractor you're considering.

Most contractors will bid a fixed price for a construction job, to be paid in installments based on the amount of work completed. Many states limit the amount of money that contractors can request before work begins. Though some contractors may want a fee based on a percentage of the cost of materials and labor, it's usually wiser to insist on a fixed-price bid. This protects you both against an unexpected rise in the cost of materials (assuming that the contractor does the buying) and against the chance that the work will take more time, adding to your labor costs. Don't be tempted to make price your only criterion for selection; reliability, quality of work, and on-time performance are also important.

Make sure you draw up a contract before starting work (*opposite*). The agreement is binding to both parties, and it minimizes problems by defining responsibilities. You can change your mind once construction starts, but remember that this usually requires a contract modification, and will probably involve both additional expense and delays.

DOING THE WORK PARTLY—OR COMPLETELY—YOURSELF

To decide whether to do the job yourself, think realistically about your skills. Can you handle a power saw? Are you willing and able to mix and cast concrete footings? Can you swing a hammer for hours on end? To build a shed—and certainly a garage—you'll have to be adept with tools and willing to work hard. The tools you'll need are discussed on the following pages. Don't be discouraged if you're missing a few; the money you'll save by doing your own work will more than cover a few additions to your toolkit. And, if you don't own the specialty tools, you can probably rent or borrow them.

Hiring help: The bigger the structure the more help you're liable to need. Building a three-car garage with living quarters is a big undertaking for a single person. If you decide to work with subcontractors, then you're the boss. On a large job, this can be a huge task—coordinating the work, arranging for permits and inspections, scheduling deliveries, and paying the subcontractors. Consider hiring a general contractor (*above*) to oversee the parts of the project that you feel least comfortable doing yourself, such as plumbing or wiring. Even if you decide to do all the work yourself, it's still helpful to invite two or three contractors to bid on the job. Their bids will help you estimate the potential savings of doing your own work, and the pros may offer invaluable input regarding the design or construction of your shed or garage.

Buying materials: Once you've estimated your materials, make a shopping list that is complete down to the last nail. To cut the costs of materials, order as many materials as possible at a single time from a single supplier; choose your supplier on the basis of competitive bids; and order materials in regularly available, standard dimensions and in quantities 5 to 10 percent greater than your estimated needs. If part of the construction is being done by a licensed contractor, he or she may arrange to purchase materials at a professional discount. Contractors with large projects nearing completion are also good sources of salvage. Make sure you check local codes before using salvaged materials.

If you're having trouble preparing a detailed materials list, someone at the local lumberyard may be able to help; remember to bring your plans with you.

Making a schedule: Think through in advance the exact sequence of procedures. Allow extra time—and money. Plan work days so you're not caught by night or bad weather. Consider how long you may need to have power and water supplies turned off.

THE ESSENTIAL TOOLKIT

The right tool for the right job is important no matter what you intend to build. It makes the work go faster and the results are invariably better than if you try to make do with an ill-equipped toolkit. These two pages display a basic collection of tools that you will need if you are going to build your own garage or shed. Always buy the best tools you can afford; they last longer and will make it easier to do good work. Cheap tools are rarely the bargain they appear to be.

Remember that it isn't necessary to buy every tool shown on these pages. If you only plan to use a reciprocating saw for a morning, for example, it doesn't make much sense to buy it; you'd probably be better off renting the tool.

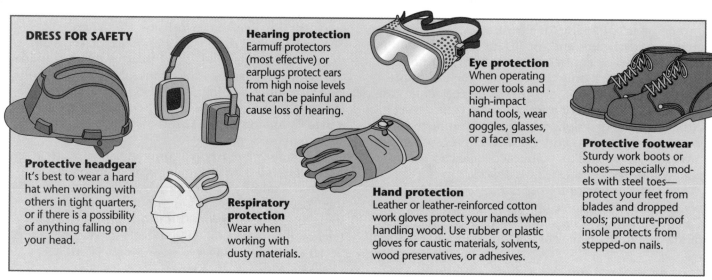

DRESS FOR SAFETY

Hearing protection
Earmuff protectors (most effective) or earplugs protect ears from high noise levels that can be painful and cause loss of hearing.

Eye protection
When operating power tools and high-impact hand tools, wear goggles, glasses, or a face mask.

Protective footwear
Sturdy work boots or shoes—especially models with steel toes—protect your feet from blades and dropped tools; puncture-proof insole protects from stepped-on nails.

Protective headgear
It's best to wear a hard hat when working with others in tight quarters, or if there is a possibility of anything falling on your head.

Respiratory protection
Wear when working with dusty materials.

Hand protection
Leather or leather-reinforced cotton work gloves protect your hands when handling wood. Use rubber or plastic gloves for caustic materials, solvents, wood preservatives, or adhesives.

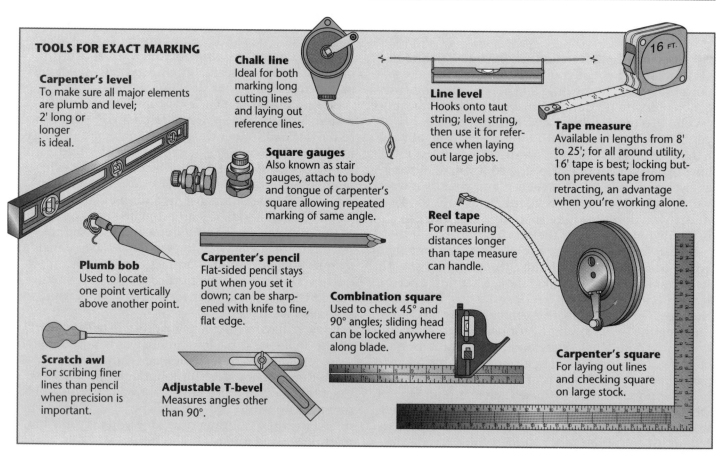

TOOLS FOR EXACT MARKING

Carpenter's level
To make sure all major elements are plumb and level; 2' long or longer is ideal.

Chalk line
Ideal for both marking long cutting lines and laying out reference lines.

Line level
Hooks onto taut string; level string, then use it for reference when laying out large jobs.

Tape measure
Available in lengths from 8' to 25'; for all around utility, 16' tape is best; locking button prevents tape from retracting, an advantage when you're working alone.

Square gauges
Also known as stair gauges, attach to body and tongue of carpenter's square allowing repeated marking of same angle.

Reel tape
For measuring distances longer than tape measure can handle.

Plumb bob
Used to locate one point vertically above another point.

Carpenter's pencil
Flat-sided pencil stays put when you set it down; can be sharpened with knife to fine, flat edge.

Combination square
Used to check 45° and 90° angles; sliding head can be locked anywhere along blade.

Carpenter's square
For laying out lines and checking square on large stock.

Scratch awl
For scribing finer lines than pencil when precision is important.

Adjustable T-bevel
Measures angles other than 90°.

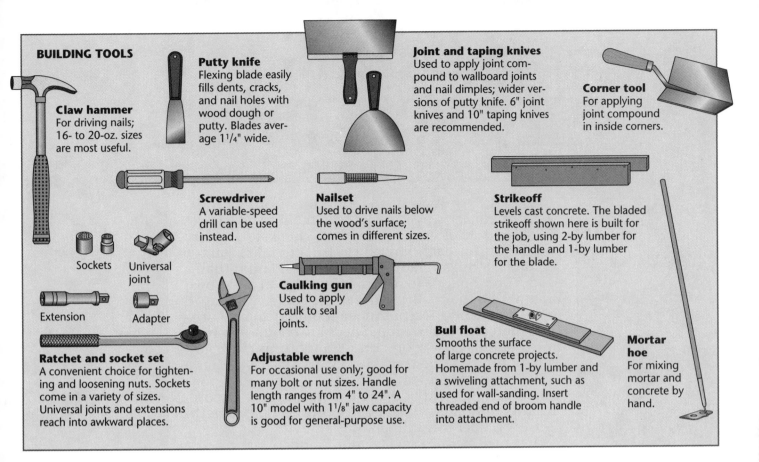

BUILDING TOOLS

Claw hammer
For driving nails; 16- to 20-oz. sizes are most useful.

Putty knife
Flexing blade easily fills dents, cracks, and nail holes with wood dough or putty. Blades average 1¼" wide.

Joint and taping knives
Used to apply joint compound to wallboard joints and nail dimples; wider versions of putty knife. 6" joint knives and 10" taping knives are recommended.

Corner tool
For applying joint compound in inside corners.

Screwdriver
A variable-speed drill can be used instead.

Nailset
Used to drive nails below the wood's surface; comes in different sizes.

Strikeoff
Levels cast concrete. The bladed strikeoff shown here is built for the job, using 2-by lumber for the handle and 1-by lumber for the blade.

Sockets

Universal joint

Extension

Adapter

Caulking gun
Used to apply caulk to seal joints.

Ratchet and socket set
A convenient choice for tightening and loosening nuts. Sockets come in a variety of sizes. Universal joints and extensions reach into awkward places.

Adjustable wrench
For occasional use only; good for many bolt or nut sizes. Handle length ranges from 4" to 24". A 10" model with 1⅛" jaw capacity is good for general-purpose use.

Bull float
Smooths the surface of large concrete projects. Homemade from 1-by lumber and a swiveling attachment, such as used for wall-sanding. Insert threaded end of broom handle into attachment.

Mortar hoe
For mixing mortar and concrete by hand.

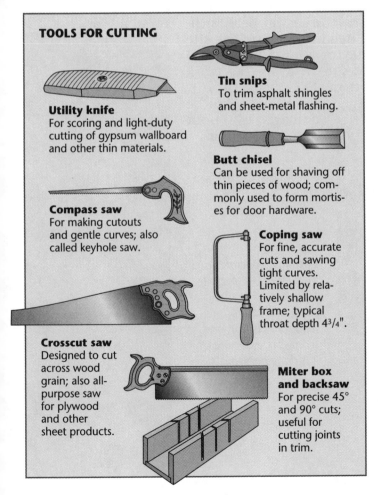

TOOLS FOR CUTTING

Utility knife
For scoring and light-duty cutting of gypsum wallboard and other thin materials.

Tin snips
To trim asphalt shingles and sheet-metal flashing.

Butt chisel
Can be used for shaving off thin pieces of wood; commonly used to form mortises for door hardware.

Compass saw
For making cutouts and gentle curves; also called keyhole saw.

Coping saw
For fine, accurate cuts and sawing tight curves. Limited by relatively shallow frame; typical throat depth 4¾".

Crosscut saw
Designed to cut across wood grain; also all-purpose saw for plywood and other sheet products.

Miter box and backsaw
For precise 45° and 90° cuts; useful for cutting joints in trim.

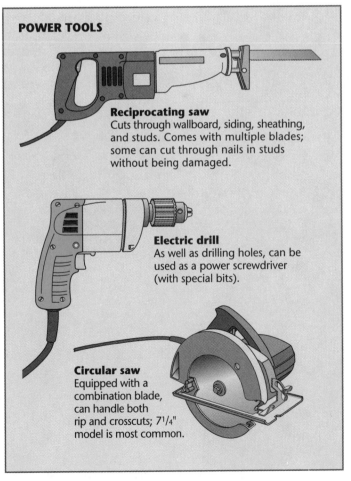

POWER TOOLS

Reciprocating saw
Cuts through wallboard, siding, sheathing, and studs. Comes with multiple blades; some can cut through nails in studs without being damaged.

Electric drill
As well as drilling holes, can be used as a power screwdriver (with special bits).

Circular saw
Equipped with a combination blade, can handle both rip and crosscuts; 7¼" model is most common.

LAYING THE GROUNDWORK

A solid, well-constructed foundation is fundamental to any structure you build—and garages and sheds are no exception. There are a variety of choices for each structure. In general, a garage requires a stronger, more elaborate foundation than a shed. Three options for a garage foundation are shown on page 33: the traditional slab on grade, a T-shaped foundation, and a recent innovation from Europe—the frost-protected foundation. Sheds are commonly built on wooden skids or on concrete footings *(page 40)*. The footings can be topped off with a pier that has a metal connector already attached. Or you can pour your own pier and add the connector you choose. Another option is to cast the footing and pier together using a fiber form tube.

Of course, before you lay your foundations you first have to determine where the building will go. This involves checking your property lines and local building code to ensure that the structure is properly situated *(page 31)*. You may also need to prepare the site to make sure that the drainage for your structure will be adequate *(page 32)*. Make sure you do this work before you begin construction. Even a well-built foundation can be damaged by a poor drainage system.

Casting a concrete foundation—especially for a large structure like a two-car garage—requires planning and teamwork to ensure that it is done properly.

SITE PREPARATION

Before you lay out the perimeter of your new structure, you need to know the precise boundaries of your building site. This will allow you to take into account any setback (the distance away from the property line) requirements as specified by local zoning ordinances.

Once the foundation has been roughly defined *(below)*, you can use the simple 3-4-5 triangulation method to ensure that the corners of the structure are square *(page 32)*. Keep in mind that this system works with any multiple of 3-4-5, such as 6-8-10, 9-12-15, or even 12-16-20. For maximum accuracy, use the largest multiple possible. As shown on the opposite page, a plumb bob can then be used to mark the exact spot in the ground where your foundation's corners will go.

Another important issue that is too often neglected for outdoor structures is drainage. For some practical drainage information, consult the tips on the following page before you begin.

Locating the footings

TOOLKIT
- Claw hammer
- Tape measure
- Carpenter's square
- Carpenter's level
- Plumb bob

1 Setting up batterboards

Using the edge of your property line or the corner of your house as a starting point, locate one corner of the shed or garage and drive a stake (A) at that point. Measure along from A—again, using the property line or the corner of your house—and drive in stake B. Use a square and a tape measure to determine the approximate locations of corners C and D. Drive in stakes at these points.

Construct batterboards from 1x2 lumber outside the corners you have staked so that a line running diagonally from B to D and from C to A would extend to the corners of the respective batterboards, as shown in the illustration below. Then stretch mason's line between the batterboards so the line is directly above A and B. Tack the line in place on the batterboards.

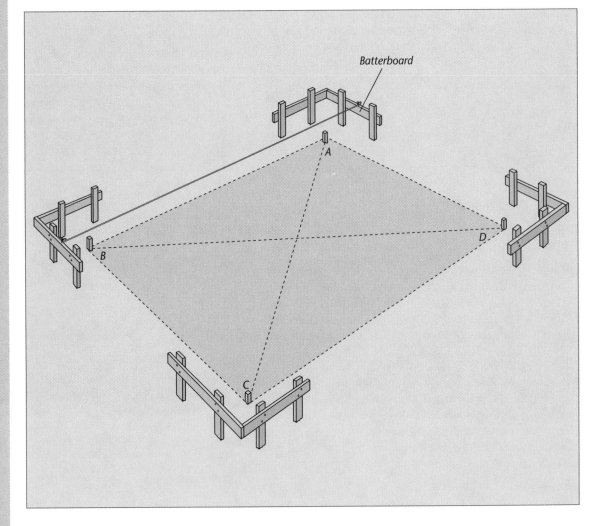

Batterboard

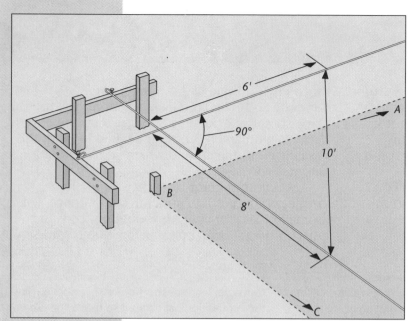

2 Refining the precise layout

Now that you have a rough layout of the foundation of your structure, you need to refine the measurements to make sure that the corners are perfectly square and the sides are the proper length. Stretch a mason's line over stakes B and C. To make sure that the angle formed by the intersection of the two lines is at 90°, measure 6' along line AB. Then put a mark on line BC 8' from B. Move the string back and forth along the batterboard until the diagonal is exactly 10', as shown at left, then secure the line in place. Repeat with the other batterboards until all the corners are square. Measure from the intersection point of the lines to set the dimensions of the building. As a final check for square, measure the diagonals; they should be equal.

3 Marking the locations of the corners

Use a plumb bob to transfer the point where the strings cross to the ground; mark the point with a small flag (drive a large nail through a piece of colored tape), a stake, or lime. Then, measure along the strings and plumb down to mark the other corners as shown; make sure your tape measure is level.

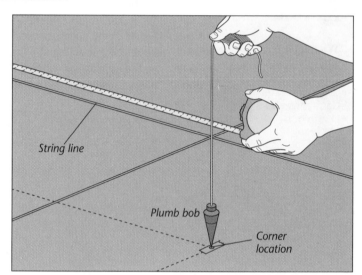

String line

Plumb bob

Corner location

ENSURING PROPER DRAINAGE

Proper drainage reduces the effects that water erosion and, in colder climates, frost heave have on your foundation. You may have to adjust the landscaping of your lot to direct water away from the structure you intend to build, sloping the ground to ensure that water does not pool near your foundation.

To draw water away from the structure itself, lay a perforated drain pipe *(right)* around the garage or shed. The pipe should rest on a bed of crushed gravel and lie below the level of the foundation. Cover the pipe with more crushed gravel, landscaping fabric, and backfill. The landscaping fabric keeps dirt from working its way down to the pipe and clogging it.

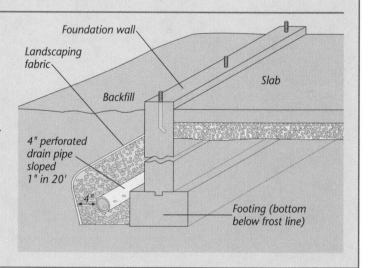

Foundation wall

Landscaping fabric

Backfill

Slab

4" perforated drain pipe sloped 1" in 20'

4"

Footing (bottom below frost line)

CONCRETE FOUNDATIONS

If you're building a garage, regardless of the type, you'll need to construct a foundation. Sheds, too, may require a foundation (*page 40*), but since they are traditionally much smaller than a garage, their requirements are not as stringent.

For many years the two principal methods of building a concrete foundation have been a slab on grade and a T-shape foundation. Recently, a Scandinavian method known as a frost-protected slab has come into use in North America.

A slab on grade is a common choice in warm climates. Basically, a slab is cast on a bed of crushed gravel with wire mesh or other reinforcing material to prevent cracking. The advantages of a slab are simplicity and cost. Placing the slab is a relatively straightforward task, although leveling—or "floating"—the surface is difficult. If you're doing it for the first time, get some experienced help; a concrete slab is permanent, and once it is poured, there is no turning back.

Traditionally, people who wanted to build garages in a cold climate chose a T-shaped foundation, which is not affected by frost. The foundation consists basically of three parts: a footing, which extends below the frost line; foundation walls, which are centered on the foot-

THREE TYPES OF FOUNDATIONS

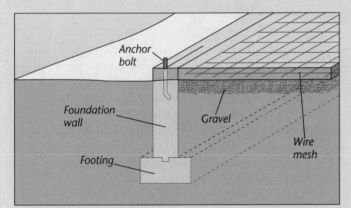

SLAB ON GRADE
As the name suggests, a slab is a single layer of concrete, several inches thick. The slab is poured thicker at the edges, to form an integral footing; reinforcing rods strengthen the thickened edge. The slab normally rests on a bed of crushed gravel to improve drainage. Casting a wire mesh in the concrete reduces the chance of cracking. A slab on grade is suitable in areas where the ground doesn't freeze, but it can also be adapted with insulation to prevent it from being affected by frost heaves (*below*).

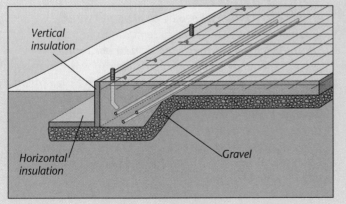

T-SHAPED
A traditional foundation method to support a structure in an area where the ground freezes. A footing is placed below the frost line and then walls are added on top. The footing is wider than the wall, providing extra support at the base of the foundation. A T-shaped foundation is normally made in three steps: first, the footing is placed and allowed to cure; second, the walls are constructed; and finally, the slab is poured between the walls.

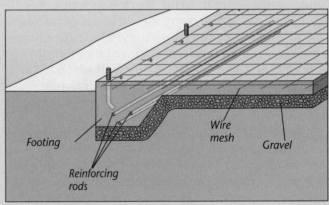

FROST PROTECTED
This method only works with a heated structure. It relies on the use of two sheets of rigid, polystyrene insulation—one on the outside of the foundation wall and the other laid flat on a bed of gravel at the base of the wall—to prevent freezing, which is a problem with slab-on-grade foundations in areas with frost. The insulation holds heat from the structure in the ground under the footings and prevents heat loss from the edge of the slab. This heat keeps the ground temperature around the footings above freezing.

ing; and a slab between the walls. Now, there is a third option, a frost-protected foundation, a slab with polystyrene insulation to prevent freezing *(page 33)*. Depending on the depth of the frost line in your area, this method can easily save you hundreds of dollars. (The frost line in North Dakota, for example, is 5 feet below ground level.) But check your building codes to see whether this method is allowed where you live.

Obviously the amount of concrete you will need depends on the size of your foundations. For a slab for a shed you may be able to mix the material yourself *(page 41)*; for a larger project, you're better off hiring a commercial ready-mix truck. Check your Yellow Pages under "Concrete—Ready Mixed."

There are two ways to attach the walls of your garage or shed to the foundation. One is to sink 1/2-inch anchor bolts into the foundation 5 to 6 inches deep; about 2 1/2 to 3 inches should protrude. The anchor bolts should be spaced no more than 6 feet apart; your plan may specify exact locations. Drill the sole plate to accept the anchor bolts and secure the plate with nuts and washers.

Another technique is to cast a 2x4—or whatever size lumber you're using for the framing—into the top of the wall or slab. Hammer angled 2 1/2-inch nails in the bottom of the 2x4s to anchor the board to the concrete. The top face of the lumber should be level with the height of the finished foundation. Tack the wood in place with duplex nails driven through the forms. Once the cement has cured, remove the nails.

A T-SHAPED FOUNDATION

The footing for a T-shaped foundation should normally be below the frost line. Check your local building codes to find out how deep this is in your area. Typical footings are equal in depth to the width of the wall, and twice as wide. Once completed, the foundation walls will then form the outside border of the floor, which is made the same way as a slab on grade but without the integral footing.

Forms for footings and walls: Forms are wooden structures that hold and mold your footing or wall. They are removed once the concrete has cured. Building forms is not difficult, but it is exacting. Concrete is dense and heavy; it exerts a lot of pressure on the forms so they must be sturdy. The instructions on the following pages give a standard method of building them; there are many others. If you have a deep frost line, you should check with a concrete plant in your area. Some companies with ready-mix trucks also rent pre-fabricated forms that can be snapped together quickly and then disassembled once your foundations have cured.

Steel reinforcing: Concrete is enormously strong in compression, resisting crushing forces of thousands of pounds per square inch. However, forces that pull, referred to as tension, can more easily break concrete.

Adding steel rods changes all this, allowing concrete to resist tension forces. Local codes specify standards for the reinforcement you'll need.

AIR-ENTRAINED CONCRETE

Adding an air-entraining agent to the concrete mix creates tiny air bubbles in the finished concrete. These help it to expand and contract without cracking, a quality important in areas with cycles of freezing and thawing. The agent also makes concrete more workable and easier to place—the extra workability means you can add less water to a batch. This makes the finished concrete stronger. An air-entraining agent should be added to ready-mix, whatever the local climate; specify this when you order. An air-entraining agent is difficult for do-it-yourselfers to find; it's not normally available at home centers, but you might be able to purchase a small amount by talking to a building contractor.

ASK A PRO

WHAT IS HYDRATION?
Hydration, a process whereby cement and water combine chemically, is the key to hardness in finished concrete. Some care must be taken to ensure that this process proceeds slowly and completely; if water is allowed to evaporate too quickly from concrete, hydration will be incomplete, and the finished concrete will be weak. To ensure that hydration will be complete, damp-curing is used. With a concrete slab, this is accomplished by covering the freshly placed slab with a plastic sheet or a spray-on curing film, or simply by keeping it wet for several days.

Making the footings

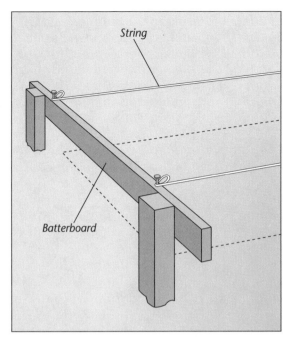

String

Batterboard

1 Laying out the footing and preparing the base

Use strings and batterboards as a guide for the footing trench. To construct the batterboard, drive in 2x2 stakes with a small hand-drilling hammer at each end of the trench and nail on 1x4s at least as wide as the trench. Attach strings to mark the edges of the trench *(left)*. You can also use these strings as guides for your forms once the trench is complete.

Because concrete needs uniform support, it should never be cast on backfilled soil. For this reason, the bottom of the trench is excavated to the correct depth. If you should happen to dig too deep, let concrete fill the excess—do not backfill. If the soil is soft, dig it out and replace it with well-tamped gravel.

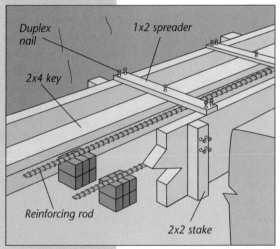

Duplex nail

1x2 spreader

2x4 key

Reinforcing rod

2x2 stake

2 Constructing a form

The easiest route to a footing is simply to dig a trench and cast concrete in the earth. In cases where the earth is too soft or too damp to hold a vertical edge, you can build a simple form, as shown at left, using the batterboard strings as a guide. Build the form from 2x10s. Both sides should be level across. Stake the side forms with 1x4 or 2x2 wood stakes no more than 4' apart. Use 3$^1/_2$" duplex nails (for easy removal) in 2" lumber or 2$^1/_2$" nails in 1" lumber. Forms are typically 16" wide.

Spreaders made of 1x2s can be nailed to the tops of the forms to keep them properly separated until the concrete is placed, then the spreaders are removed for striking. A 2x4 key nailed under the spreader in the middle of the trench will also be removed as soon as the concrete holds its shape. (The key will help tie the footing and walls together.)

Place steel reinforcing rods on pieces of brick, stone, or broken concrete one-half of the footing's thickness up from the bottom of the trench.

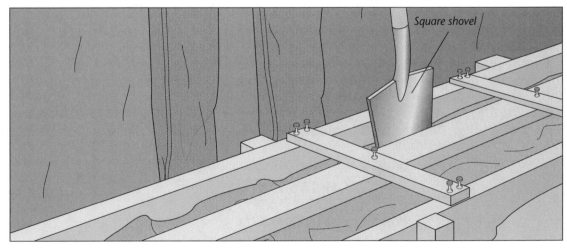

Square shovel

3 Placing the concrete

Coat the insides of the form with form-release agent so it can later be separated from the concrete and removed. Then, place the concrete for the footing, compacting it firmly with a shovel.

Run the shovel up and down along the edges of the forms to ensure that no voids are left. In placement and compacting, always work systematically from one end of the footing to the other.

4 ▶ Striking off

First, remove the spreaders. Use a piece of wood to strike the concrete level with the top of the form. Work with a zigzag motion from one end to the other, knocking down high spots and filling any hollows. Once the concrete can hold its shape, remove the key.

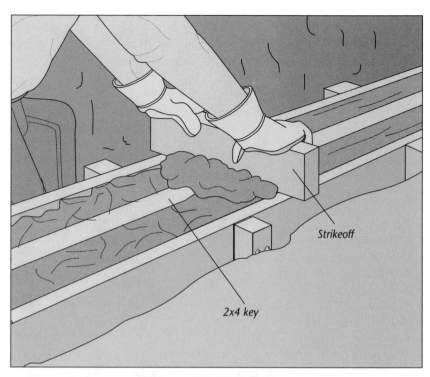

Strikeoff

2x4 key

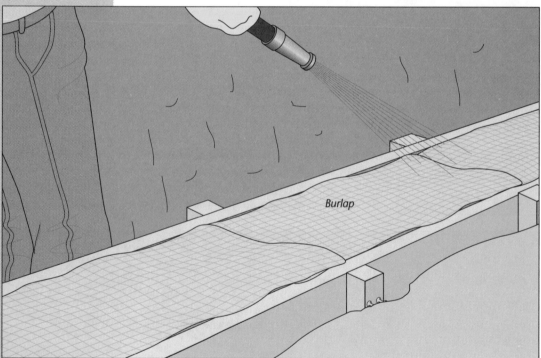

Burlap

◀ 5 Curing the concrete

After striking, the footing should be cured for 7 days; the longer the cure, the stronger the concrete. Cover it with burlap, damp sand, plastic sheeting, or a spray-on curing compound available from your masonry supplier. Keep the porous coverings wet to ensure hydration: Spray them several times a day, especially if the weather is hot and dry. Once curing is complete, remove the forms.

 PLAY IT SAFE

WORKING WITH CONCRETE
Always wear safety goggles when working with concrete. Wet concrete is caustic, so wear gloves to protect your hands. Also wear rubber boots if you're going to have to walk in the concrete to strike it off. If wet concrete comes in contact with your skin—including through clothing—wash thoroughly with water.

Building foundation walls

TOOLKIT
- Circular saw
- Claw hammer
- Hand-drilling hammer
- Square shovel
- Tamper (optional)
- Lumber for strikeoff
- Wire cutters
- Electric drill

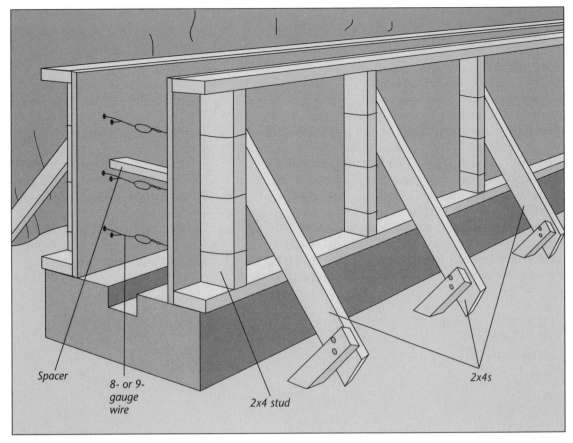

Spacer

8- or 9-gauge wire

2x4 stud

2x4s

1 Building forms on footing

Once the footings have cured, it is time to construct the forms for the walls. If you need to build long forms, do it in sections of no more than 8'. For each section, build a frame of 2x4s as shown above, then attach the sheathing—either ½-inch or ⅜-inch plywood.

Drill holes next to the studs every two feet or so for 8- or 9-gauge wire. Wrap the wire around opposing studs and secure it together between the sides of the forms. Place a stick between the wires inside the forms and twist the wire tight like a tourniquet. Cut 1x2 or 2x4 spacers to the width of the walls and place them next to the wires as shown *(above)*.

Tighten the wires until the spacers are held in place; this will ensure that the walls will be the same width from top to bottom. Tie pull wires on the spacers you will not be able to reach once you begin placing the concrete. (The spacers need to be removed as you go.) Place the forms on the footing and nail the sections together. Then plumb the structure and brace it with 2x4s.

2 Casting the wall

Place the concrete and strike it just as you did for the footing *(page 35)*. When you've filled the forms close to the top, set anchor bolts in the concrete, about 6' apart, so that 2½" to 3" of the bolt is exposed.

With the footings and the walls completed, place the concrete slab that will form the floor between the walls *(page 38)*.

A CONCRETE SLAB

Making a concrete slab is similar to pouring a slab between a T-shaped foundation *(page 33)*. Both should be at least 4 inches thick. The difference is that the edges of a freestanding slab are thicker, or "turned down." This thickening—roughly 8 inches deep and 1 foot wide—acts as an integral footing, anchoring the slab. This isn't necessary with the T-shaped foundation because the walls serve the same purpose. A turned down slab's top should be at least 6 inches above grade.

Concrete requires a stable, well-drained base that gives it uniform support. Because the finished slab is monolithic, it's especially important to ensure that the ground beneath it doesn't shift and cause the concrete to crack.

Generally, a layer of welded-wire mesh is positioned in the forms, and the concrete is cast over and around it. This steel mesh provides reinforcement and helps prevent cracking. Another way to prevent cracking, called jointing, is discussed opposite.

Before building the forms for the slab and placing the concrete you need to level the site. You also need to install any plumbing service lines *(page 23)*.

When placing the concrete, divide your work into smaller stages. Cast large slabs in sections using a wet screed–a patch of concrete placed and leveled to separate the work area into manageable sections. Placing concrete is a big job, consider hiring a professional.

Casting a monolithic slab

TOOLKIT
- Circular saw
- Claw hammer
- Bolt cutters or heavy pliers
- Carpenter's level
- Square shovel
- Mortar hoe
- Lumber for strike-off
- Darby or bull float
- Wheelbarrow

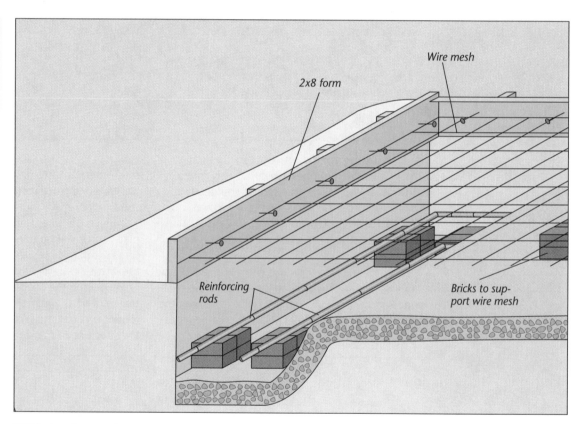

2x8 form

Wire mesh

Reinforcing rods

Bricks to support wire mesh

1 Casting in the forms

Construct forms around the perimeter of the site from 2x8 lumber, bracing them securely. The tops of the forms should be level; for the sake of drainage, you can also slant them by 1" in 20'.

Install six-inch-square No.10-10 welded-wire mesh between the forms, keeping it at least 1½" from the sides. The mesh can be cut with bolt cutters or heavy pliers and supported on bits of brick.

Just before placing your concrete, go over your forms to check for level (or grade) and to be sure everything is secure. Forms should be coated with form-release agent to aid in removal.

Thoroughly dampen the soil or gravel. Start placing the concrete for the wet screed down the middle of the slab area. Have a helper spread it with a shovel or hoe. Work the concrete up against the form with a square shovel or mortar hoe; with a hoe, push—don't drag—the concrete and don't spread it too far; overworking will force the heavy aggregate to the bottom and bring up small particles that can cause defects in the finished concrete. Instead, space out your placement along the length of the area, working each batch just enough to form a continuous wet screed.

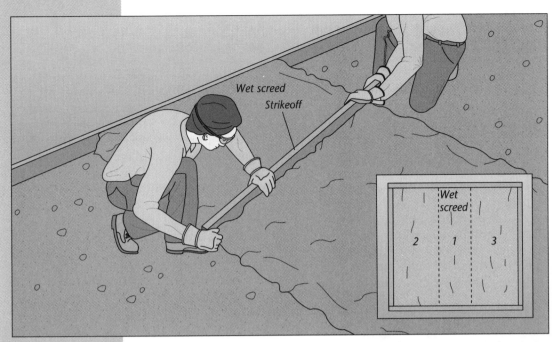

Wet screed
Strikeoff

Wet screed

2 | 1 | 3

2 ► **Striking the concrete**
With a helper, slowly move a strikeoff (in this case a straight 2x4) across the wet screed to level it, using a zigzag, sawing motion. From time to time, lay a carpenter's level on your strikeoff to check for level across the wet screed. Also check that the top of the wet screed is level with the form board. If needed, a third person can shovel extra concrete into any remaining low points.

3 ► **Smoothing**
After striking the concrete, use a darby or a bull float—depending on the size of your project—for the initial finishing. Smooth down any high spots and fill any small hollows. Use the darby on small projects; move it in overlapping arcs, then repeat with overlapping straight, side-to-side strokes. Keep the tool flat, but don't let it dig in. For larger jobs, use a bull float *(right)*. Push it away from you with its leading edge raised slightly. Pull it back nearly flat; overlap your passes. Put a final finish on the slab with a wood float. If a slick smooth surface is desired, follow with a steel trowel. Cure the slab *(page 36)*.

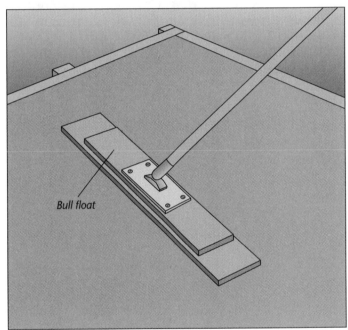

Bull float

ASK A PRO

JOINTING A SLAB

Joints are used to prevent irregular cracking of concrete by allowing the concrete to crack in straight lines at predetermined locations.

Control joints are tooled into the wet concrete with a jointer during finishing. The distance between joints should not exceed 30 times the thickness of a slab—10' apart for a 4" slab.

Isolation joints, on the other hand, are used wherever a new slab adjoins previous construction. They allow independent movement of the structures. From a dealer, buy special ½-inch-thick 4-inch-wide asphalt-impregnated isolation-joint strips in 8- or 10-foot lengths and put in place before casting the concrete against them.

FOUNDATIONS FOR SHEDS

Although sheds, like some garages, may be built on slab foundations, many have built-up floors that rest on wooden skids or concrete footings and piers *(below)*.

For large jobs, it's usually easier to have concrete delivered pre-mixed, but pier foundations require relatively small amounts of concrete so you should be able to mix it yourself *(opposite)*.

For sheds with wooden skid foundations, choose foundation-grade pressure-treated lumber to prevent moisture decay caused by ground contact. The rim joists are then nailed along the top of the skids, with the floor joists spanning between the rim joists and the two skids.

The shed's flooring can be constructed from sheets of ¾-inch exterior-grade plywood. For extra strength, you may choose to use tongue-and-groove exterior grade plywood. In either case, nail the flooring in place with 2-inch nails every 6 inches at the edge of the plywood sheets and every 10 inches along the intermediate joists.

Drainage is important with this kind of shed. Remove 4 to 6 inches of earth from the spot where you will construct the shed. Then replace the earth with a 4-inch layer of pea gravel beneath your shed. Another option is to dig a drainage trench approximately 12 inches wide and 6 inches deep where the 4x8 skids are to be placed. Fill the trench with gravel to ensure good drainage while minimizing contact with soil.

Concrete footings and piers are identical to the foundation commonly used to support a deck. The most common options are a precast concrete pier embedded in a concrete footing; a concrete pier poured on top of a concrete footing; and a footing and pier cast together—usually with the help of a fiber form tube. Once the piers are in place, 4x6 beams are placed in the metal anchors and tied together by 2x8 joists. Rim joists (2x8s) cover the joists' ends and strengthen the structure. The layout for the piers is much the same as for footings and slabs *(page 31)*.

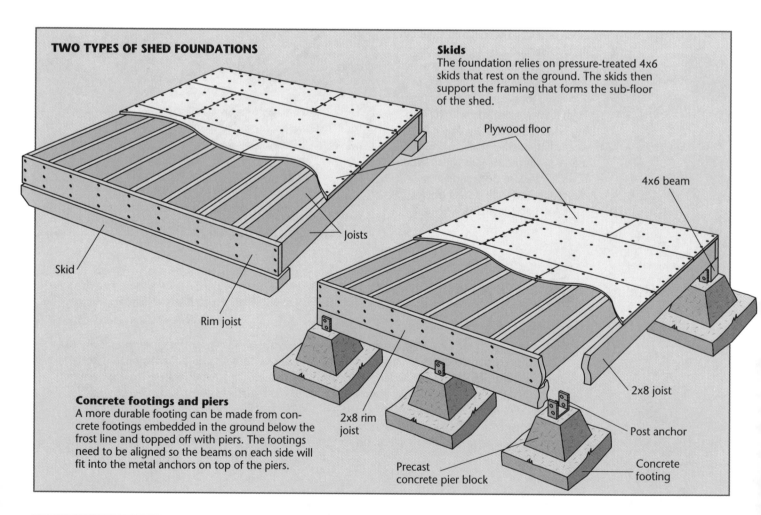

TWO TYPES OF SHED FOUNDATIONS

Skids
The foundation relies on pressure-treated 4x6 skids that rest on the ground. The skids then support the framing that forms the sub-floor of the shed.

Plywood floor

4x6 beam

Joists

Skid

Rim joist

Concrete footings and piers
A more durable footing can be made from concrete footings embedded in the ground below the frost line and topped off with piers. The footings need to be aligned so the beams on each side will fit into the metal anchors on top of the piers.

2x8 rim joist

2x8 joist

Post anchor

Precast concrete pier block

Concrete footing

WORKING WITH CONCRETE

If you've chosen to mix concrete yourself, you can make your own batch from scratch *(below)* or buy prepackaged mix, which only requires water. The latter option is more expensive, so you should compare costs when you plan. In either case, be prepared for a day of hard work; there's nothing like working with concrete to test your stamina.

Concrete can be mixed in a wheelbarrow or a mortar box, or if larger quantities are required, you can rent a concrete mixer from a tool rental agency. Get exact instructions on how to use the machine before you start. You'll want a square shovel to measure the concrete ingredients.

Be sure to wash your tools with water, as soon as you have finished with them. Once concrete has begun to cure, it is very difficult to remove.

Wet concrete is caustic, so take precautions such as wearing heavy work gloves.

A CONCRETE FORMULA

All proportions are by volume. The sand should be clean concrete sand (never beach sand); the aggregate should range in size from quite small to about ¾ inch in size. The water should be drinkable—neither excessively alkaline nor acidic, nor containing organic matter.

The following is a good formula to use for concrete footings:

1 part portland cement
2½ parts sand
2½ parts stone or gravel aggregate
½ part water

To know how much concrete to buy, refer to the table at right. The figures given are for 10 cubic feet of finished concrete and include 10% extra for waste. Note that the final volume is less than the sum of the ingredients because the smaller particles fit in among the larger ones. If you order bulk materials sold by the cubic yard, remember that each cubic yard contains 27 cubic feet.

INGREDIENTS FOR 10 CUBIC FEET OF CONCRETE	
Bulk dry materials	Portland cement: 2.6 sacks Sand: 5.8 sacks Aggregate: 6.5 cubic feet
Dry prepackaged mix	20 60-pound bags
Ready-mix	.41 cubic yards

Mixing concrete by hand

TOOLKIT
- Square shovel
- Mortar hoe
- Wheelbarrow or mortar box
- Pail

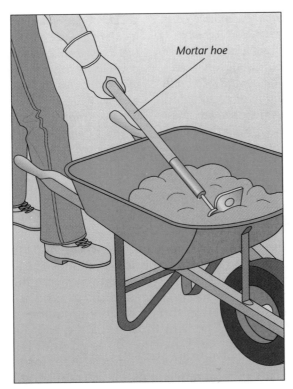

Mortar hoe

Using a mortar hoe
To measure out the ingredients, use shovelfuls for the dry ingredients. Use a pail for the water after finding out how many shovelfuls it takes to fill your pail.

First, spread the sand and cement on the mixing surface. Using a rolling motion, mix these ingredients until the color is even. Add the aggregate; again, mix until the color is even. Finally, scoop out a hole in the middle of the dry ingredients and add the water.

Work around the edges of the puddle with the hoe or shovel, slowly rolling the dry ingredients into the water. Take particular care not to slop the water out of the wheelbarrow (or off the platform), since escaping water may weaken the batch by carrying particles of cement with it.

Work in small batches; this will make mixing easier and give you more control over proportions.

Mixing concrete by machine

TOOLKIT
- Carpenter's level
- Square shovel
- Concrete mixer

Using a concrete mixer

Set up the mixer close to your supplies of sand and aggregate so you can feed the machine directly from the piles. Wedge the machine firmly in place and make sure it's level. CAUTION: Concrete mixers can be dangerous—read the safety information below.

First, with the mixer off, add the coarse aggregate and half the water. Then, turn on the machine to scour the drum. (If the machine is gas-powered, you'll need to warm it up.) Next, add the sand, and all but about 10% of the water. Then, add the portland cement. When the mixture is an even color and consistency, add the rest of the water. Mix for at least 2 minutes or until the mixture has reached a uniform appearance.

Measure the dry ingredients by equal shovelfuls as you add them; never put the shovel inside the mixer while it's in operation.

Concrete mixer

PLAY IT SAFE

WORKING WITH A CONCRETE MIXER

Be sure to follow all the safety measures for the concrete mixer you're using. Never reach into a rotating mixer drum with your hands or tools. Wear tight-fitting clothes, a dust mask, and goggles, and keep away from the moving parts. Do not look into the mixer while it's running—check the mix by dumping some out.

Mixers are either electric or gas-powered. To avoid shock hazard, an electric mixer must be plugged into a ground-fault circuit interrupter (GFCI) outlet. The mixer should have a three-prong grounding-type plug; use only an outdoor-rated three-prong extension cord.

Do not run an electric mixer in wet or damp conditions and be sure to cover it with a tarpaulin when not in use.

The engine on a gasoline-powered mixer should be fueled from the proper type of can for storing and pouring flammable fuel. Add fuel only when the engine is off and has cooled down; close the fuel container tightly after fueling. Any fuel spills should be wiped up immediately. While the engine is running, don't work or stand where you must breathe the exhaust fumes. And never run the mixer in an enclosed space.

CASTING FOOTINGS AND PIERS

The simplest method for building foundations is to cast a footing and set a precast concrete pier block on top of it *(opposite)*. You can also cast your own piers by building a form on top of the footing and placing the concrete in it. One advantage of this method is that you'll have a greater choice of post anchors. In areas with substantial rain or standing water, for example, builders typically choose a post anchor that allows a slight clearance between the

concrete and the wood. Adjustable bases allow the beam to be adjusted once the anchor is in place.

In a cold climate, it's very important to sink the footings deep in the ground. The bottoms of the footings should be about 6 inches below the frost line, to prevent the foundation from shifting with freezing and thawing of the ground. The easiest way to do this is to use commercial fiber form tubes, which come in a range of diameters and lengths.

When casting footings or piers, you may need to add steel bars for reinforcement. Requirements for steel reinforcement are governed by the building codes in effect in your area.

In general, footings must be cast on solid, undisturbed soil, but in some areas gravel is required below the footing for drainage; again, check the codes in your area. Before mixing the concrete, remove the string lines that define the location of the footings and dig the holes to the depth required by code—usually 6 inches below the frost line. Cast the concrete, then replace the string lines to align the pier blocks or post anchors.

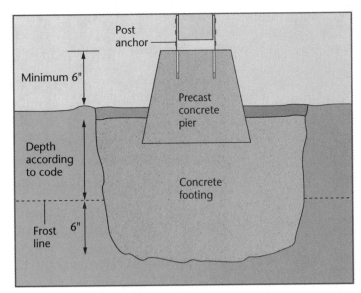

Casting footings and adding piers

TOOLKIT
- Mortar hoe or shovel for placing concrete
- Carpenter's level

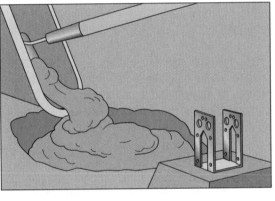

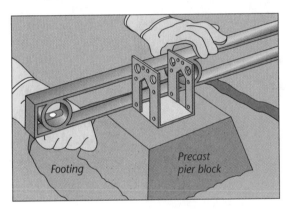

Using precast piers
First soak the pier blocks with a hose. Then cast the footings to the depth and size required by the local building code *(above, left)*; the top of the footing should be about 1" below grade. Wait a few min-utes—until the concrete has stiffened enough to support the piers—then position the pier blocks and level them in both directions *(above, right)*. Cover the exposed part of the footings with earth.

Casting footings and piers together

TOOLKIT
- Tape measure
- Crosscut saw
- Mortar hoe or shovel for placing concrete
- Claw hammer
- Carpenter's level
- Shovel

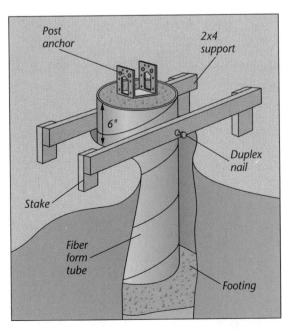

Using fiber form tubes
The hole for the fiber form tube must be splayed at the bottom to allow the concrete to spread out to form a footing. Cut the tube to length and suspend it; it should be about 6" above the bottom of the hole and extend at least 6" above grade. Hold the tube at the right height by nailing a staked 2x4 laid on edge to each side of the tube using duplex nails as shown.

Insert steel rods if necessary and place the concrete. Smooth off the top with a piece of wood and immediately insert a metal post anchor; align it using the string lines. Make sure the anchor is level by inserting a piece of beam material in the anchor and checking it for plumb with a carpenter's level.

Fill in the hole around the tube with earth. Cover the top of the tube with newspaper, straw, or burlap and keep it damp for at least a week. Then peel off the part of the tube that sticks up above the ground.

FRAMING THE STRUCTURE

The first glimpse of how your new shed or garage will look happens once the framing process begins. It's at that time, when the outlines of the walls and roof and the openings for the windows and doors begin to appear, that the various building materials come together in the semblance of a real structure.

Featured in this chapter is platform framing, the most common building technique used in construction today. When building a house using this type of framing, the walls rise from the subfloor. In a typical garage, they begin at the slab.

Beginning with the drilling of the holes for the sole plate on top of the foundation *(opposite)*, this chapter will show you how to solidly build walls and secure them in place. To create openings for doors (including garage doors) and windows, turn to the instructions beginning on page 47.

Information for sheathing the wall, as well as cutting openings for windows and doors, raising the wall, making it plumb, and anchoring it in place, starts on page 49.

Once the walls are up, roof and ceiling framing comes next. To learn about installing roof rafters and ceiling joists, turn to page 52. Finally, finishing the roof, as well as a discussion of different roof shapes for sheds and garages, begins on page 57.

Once you've cut the openings in the sheathing for your windows and doors, you'll need a few helpers to raise the structure and secure it in place. See page 51 for more details.

WALL FRAMING

There are a few steps to follow when framing the walls of your shed or garage: Assemble the components on the ground; raise each section into position, checking it for plumb and bracing it securely; and fasten individual sections to the foundation and to each other. Long exterior walls should be raised first, then tie in the end walls and add any interior walls. Framing requires a sole plate, wall studs, a top plate, and, sometimes, horizontal fire blocks between studs. Doorways or window openings need headers to span the opening and extra studs.

Usually, garages are framed to the same structural standards as a house. Traditionally, walls were built from 2x4 studs and plates, with studs placed on 16-inch centers. In recent years, concern with energy-efficiency has led to higher R-value recommendations (a rating based on resistance of insulation material to heat flow)

than are possible with 2x4 walls. Many builders responded by framing exterior walls with 2x6s, which allow for more insulation. In a one-story structure, 2x6 studs can usually be placed on 24-inch centers.

Walls are classified as either bearing (supporting the weight of the structure) or nonbearing. If you want interior walls solely to divide space—to enclose a work area, for example—you can build according to the requirements for nonbearing walls: 2x4s on 24-inch centers are the norm.

The overall height of the walls should be enough to accommodate gypsum wallboard panels installed vertically, with at least a ¾-inch space on top for the ceiling panels. This height is normally factored into building plans. If you plan to enclose the walls and ceiling with wallboard, install the ceiling panels first *(page 93)*.

Preparing the sole plate

TOOLKIT
- Tape measure
- Chalk line
- Combination square
- Electric drill and bit slightly bigger than anchor bolt

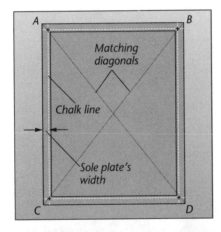

1 Checking the foundation for square
Even the best foundation may be slightly askew in the corners or a trifle long on one side; rather than follow a flaw, it's important to lay the sole plates square. To check for square, measure the diagonals between opposite corners *(left)*; the lengths of AD and BC must match exactly. Also check the measurements of the foundation against your planned dimensions.

If your measurements don't agree, mark the offending corners (for example, long ½" or short ¼"). Measure the sole plate's width and mark this distance in from each edge at the corners—adding or subtracting for any discrepancies. Snap a chalk line between each pair of marks for the inside edge of each sole plate, keeping it flush with the outside edge of the foundation wall.

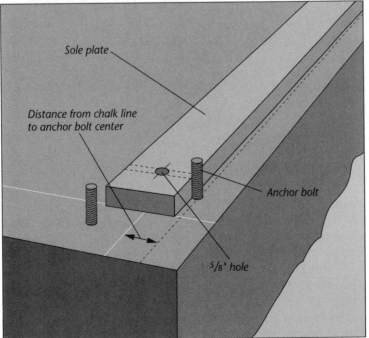

2 Drilling holes for anchor bolts
Choose the longest, straightest pressure-treated sole plate material you can find. Hold the first piece against the anchor bolts embedded in the foundation wall and use a square to transfer the location of each bolt to the sole plate. To locate the bolt hole on the sole plate's width, measure the distance from the chalk line to the center of each bolt; mark this on the sole plate. Remove the sole plate and drill slightly oversize holes (about ⅝" for a standard ½" diameter anchor bolt) through it. Repeat this procedure for each length of sole plate material you require.

Assembling a basic wall

TOOLKIT
- Circular saw
- Tape measure
- Combination square
- Framing square (optional)
- Claw hammer
- Chalk line

1 Marking the plates

Cut the top plates to length. If you need more than one piece, locate the joints at stud centers; offset any joints that lie between the top and sole plates by at least 4'. Now lay the top plate against the sole plate on the slab, and beginning at one end, measure in 1½"—the thickness of a stud—from one end and draw a line across both plates with pencil and combination square for the end studs. Starting once more from that end, measure and draw lines at 15¼" and 16¾", for studs on 16" centers (or 23¼" and 24¾" for 24" centers). From these lines, con-

tinue marking lines at 16" (or 24") intervals until you reach the far end of both plates *(below)*—most good tape measures have marks every 16" for stud placement.

You may find that an easier method is to use a framing square; you can use the tongue's thickness (1½") to mark one side of the studs, and its length (16") to position them. Note that you don't have to mark both sides of the stud positions, as shown in the illustration. Most carpenters mark one side consistently, and put a rough "X" on the side of the line where the stud goes.

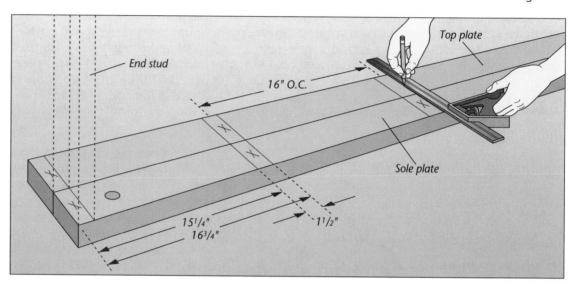

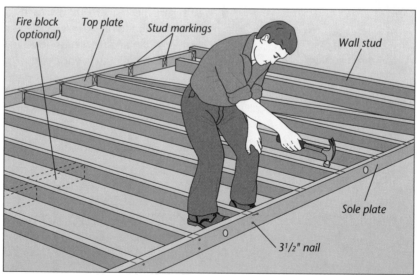

2 Assembling the pieces

Unless you're using precut studs, measure and cut the wall studs to length. Spread the plates apart and turn them on edge, stud markings inward. Place the studs between the lines and face-nail them through each plate with two 3½" nails. (Don't put full-length studs within spaces planned for doors and windows.) If fire blocks are required, center them 4' above the bottom of the sole plate.

Snap a chalk line across the studs and stagger alternate blocks slightly so you can face-nail through the studs into the fire block, rather than toenailing.

For a door or window, check the manufacturer's "rough opening" dimensions and mark the center line on the plates. Or, measure the unit and add ⅜" on the sides and top for windows, or ½" at top and sides for doors. The extra space is for shims.

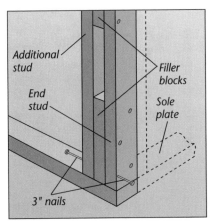

Additional stud
End stud
Filler blocks
Sole plate
3" nails

3 Framing corners

Where walls meet, you need extra studs. After a long exterior wall is assembled, add extra studs at both ends; space them away from end studs with filler blocks (left). Nail through both studs into each block with 3" nails.

If walls will be covered with plywood siding or sheathing or diagonally laid solid lumber, you may not need to brace exterior walls. Any other materials require diagonal bracing—let-in 1x4s or steel straps—at all corners and every 25' along a wall. Notch (for 1x4s) or groove (for ribbed straps) wall framing for the bracing; fasten either type to each stud or plate with two 2½" nails.

ASK A PRO

HOW DO I MAKE A SOLID JOINT BETWEEN AN INTERIOR WALL AND AN EXTERIOR WALL?

When joining interior walls to exterior walls, it's important to provide solid support. To do this, plan to add extra studs where the interior wall ties in, or meets, the exterior wall. As shown in the illustration at right, you can use three studs—a spacer stud sandwiched by two wall studs—or two studs and filler blocks. Nail the outside studs to the spacer using 3½" nails.

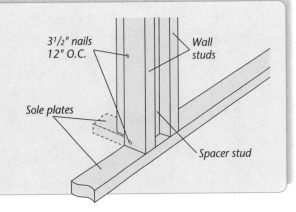

3½" nails 12" O.C.
Wall studs
Sole plates
Spacer stud

Rough window framing

TOOLKIT
• Tape measure
• Claw hammer
• Circular saw
• Combination square

Installing a rough sill and cripples

To begin window framing, place king studs as described for door framing, on page 48; nail the king studs to both plates. Ideally, the tops of all doors and windows should be the same height (typically 6'8"), so that the bottom edges of the headers match. Mark the height of the bottom of the header on the window opening's king studs. Working down from the mark, subtract the height of the rough opening. This indicates the top of the rough sill. Subtract another 1½" for the sill's thickness and make another mark. The remaining distance to the top of the sole plate equals the height of the lower cripple studs.

Cut the lower studs to length, then nail the outside pair to the king studs with 3" nails. Cut the sill and attach it to the king studs with 3½" nails. Add remaining lower cripples and the trimmer studs on each side. Finally, install the header and upper cripple studs as described for door framing.

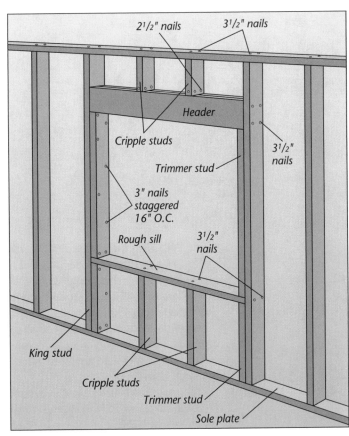

2½" nails
3½" nails
Header
Cripple studs
Trimmer stud
3½" nails
3" nails staggered 16" O.C.
Rough sill
3½" nails
King stud
Cripple studs
Trimmer stud
Sole plate

Installing rough door framing

TOOLKIT
• Tape measure
• Claw hammer
• Circular saw

1 ▶ Framing rough door openings

To frame for doors, you'll need king studs, trimmers, a header (made up of 2 boards and a spacer), and cripple studs. (See the opposite page for help on how to frame garage door openings). Measure half the rough opening width in each direction from the centerline, and draw a line to mark the inside edge of each trimmer stud. Mark off both trimmer studs and king studs on the plates, then nail the king studs to the plates. Next, cut and install the trimmer studs: Trimmer height equals the rough opening height plus the thickness of the floor and underlayment (if any). Subtract the $1^{1}/_{2}$" thickness of the sole plate and cut the trimmers to this length. Nail them to the king studs with 3" nails in a staggered pattern (right).

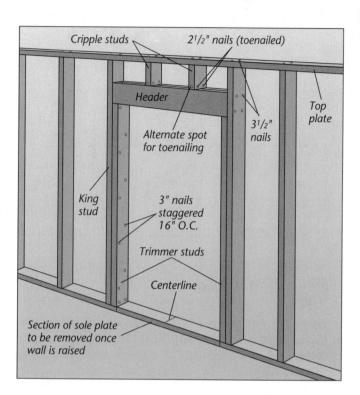

Cripple studs — $2^{1}/_{2}$" nails (toenailed) — Header — Top plate — Alternate spot for toenailing — $3^{1}/_{2}$" nails — King stud — 3" nails staggered 16" O.C. — Trimmer studs — Centerline — Section of sole plate to be removed once wall is raised

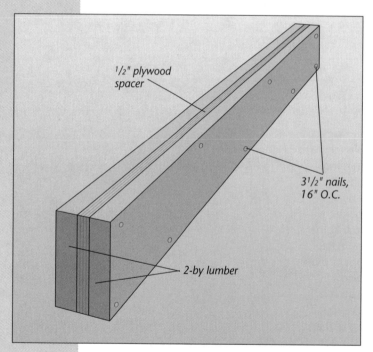

$^{1}/_{2}$" plywood spacer — $3^{1}/_{2}$" nails, 16" O.C. — 2-by lumber

MINIMUM HEADER SIZES	
Opening width	**Header size**
Up to 4'	4x4 or two 2x4s on edge
4' to 6'	4x6 or two 2x6s on edge
6' to 8'	4x8 or two 2x8s on edge
8' to 10'	4x10 or two 2x10s on edge
10' to 12'	4x12 or two 2x12s on edge

Note: Sizes are for 2x4 stud walls in single-story structures. If there's a second story above, choose the next larger header size.

2 Making and installing headers

Headers for 2x4 bearing walls are typically composed of matching lengths of 2-by lumber turned on edge, with a $^{1}/_{2}$" plywood spacer sandwiched between them. The exact depth of the required header depends on the width of your opening, and on your local building code. For a quick reference, common header sizes are listed in the chart shown at right above.

To assemble a header, cut 2-bys and plywood to the length between king studs. Nail the pieces together with $3^{1}/_{2}$" nails spaced 16" apart along both top and bottom edges (left, above). For 2x6 walls, make a $5^{1}/_{2}$" thick header by using three 2-bys and two pieces of plywood. A partition wall header may also be a single 2x4 or 2x6 laid flat across the opening. Place the header snugly on top of the trimmers and nail it through the king studs, using $3^{1}/_{2}$" nails. Measure and cut cripple studs to length. If it's possible, use the same 16" spacing as standard studs. Nail the cripple studs through the top plate, using $3^{1}/_{2}$" nails; then toenail the bottoms to the header with $2^{1}/_{2}$" nails.

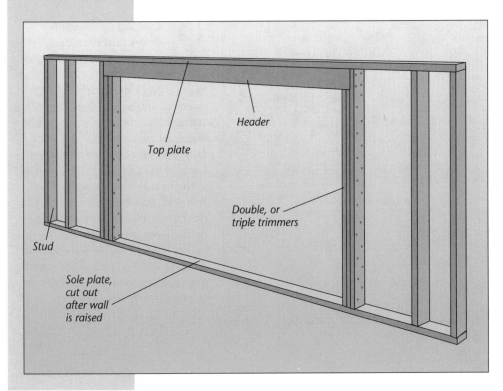

Header

Top plate

Double, or triple trimmers

Stud

Sole plate, cut out after wall is raised

Garage door openings

Although the general idea for framing a garage door is similar to framing a regular door—follow the tips on the opposite page for marking the opening—the framing needs to be more substantial. Your local building code will determine whether you need to use double or triple trimmer studs. For the header, two 2x12s with plywood may be acceptable, or you may need a glued laminated beam (glulam)—engineered structural lumber designed to span the width. Garage door openings are typically 16' to 18' wide. The header is usually nailed directly to the top plate to provide adequate clearance.

Sheathing the walls

TOOLKIT
• Tape measure
• Claw hammer
• Chalk line
• Electric drill
• Circular saw
• Reciprocating saw

1 Checking for square
With your wall framed and lying down on the slab, check to make sure the corner-to-corner measurements (diagonals) are equal. With a helper, run a tape measure from one corner of the frame to the opposite diagonal corner; repeat the measurement for the other two corners. The wall is square when the two numbers match up. If the distance is off, adjust the frame until the totals are equal. Chances are, you'll need to make slight adjustments to bring the wall square. To keep the wall in alignment, add 4x8 plywood sheathing (below) or let-in bracing (page 50) before raising it into position.

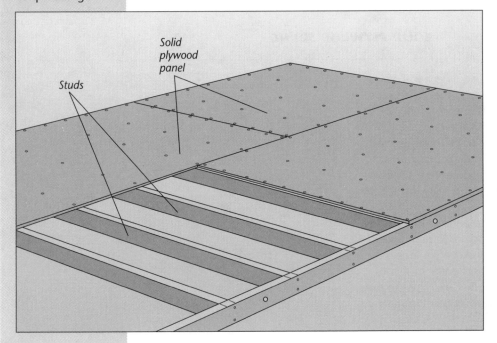

Solid plywood panel

Studs

2 Adding sheathing
Before nailing the sheathing in place, check your local building code for proper nail size and spacing requirements in your area. In the illustration at left, the plywood panels are nailed horizontally with 2" galvanized nails spaced 6" apart around the perimeter and 12" apart along the studs. Secure the first full panel to one corner of the frame, nailing along its perimeter. Before installing the second panel, saw a few feet off its length making sure that the sawed end is centered on a stud. (This will stagger the joint from the sole plate to the top plate, making for a stronger wall.) Install the remaining panels, leaving a 1/16" expansion gap between each, which can later be caulked.

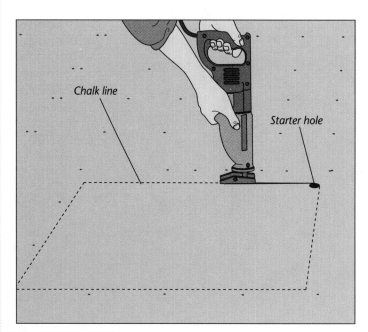

Chalk line

Starter hole

3 Cutting openings for doors and windows

To cut openings in the sheathing for windows and doors, use a reciprocating saw. Mark the location of each opening with a chalk line. Then drill a starter hole in one corner of the outline; the hole's diameter should be large enough to accommodate the blade of the saw. Insert the saw blade in the hole and cut along the chalk line *(left)*. Round off the corners, planning to cut them square once the cutout is removed. If the blade is longer than the combined width of the stud and thickness of the sheathing, prop up one corner of the wall to provide sufficient clearance.

ASK A PRO

DO I HAVE TO USE SHEATHING?

Applying sheathing is the most common method of keeping walls square, but there are other options; let-in bracing, as shown at right, for example. With this technique, 1x4 bracing is recessed, or let-in, into the studs and sole and top plates. Cut a 1x4 to fit diagonally from the top plate at one corner to the sole plate, at a 45° angle. Mark where the brace crosses the studs and meets the sole and top plates. Cut recesses at the marks so the brace sits flush with the edge of the studs and the two plates and cut the ends flush with the outside faces of the plates. Install braces at each corner, and every 25' on long walls.

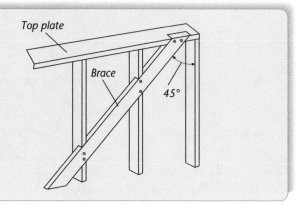

Top plate

Brace

45°

SOLID PLYWOOD SIDING

Solid plywood siding, shown at right, squares a wall and adds a decorative finish at the same time. The siding must be at least ⅜ inch thick for studs on 16-inch centers, and at least ½ inch thick for studs on 24-inch centers.

Generally, plywood siding is made to be mounted vertically, which minimizes the number of horizontal joints. If you choose to mount it horizontally, however, stagger the vertical end joints such as for installing plywood sheathing *(page 49)*.

The nails should be long enough to penetrate the studs by 1½ inches. Use 2-inch nails for ⅜-inch or ½-inch panels, and 2½-inch nails for ⅝-inch panels. Nail every 6 inches around the perimeter of each sheet, and every 12 inches along the studs. Use galvanized nails. Be careful not to dimple the wood surface with the last blow of the hammer.

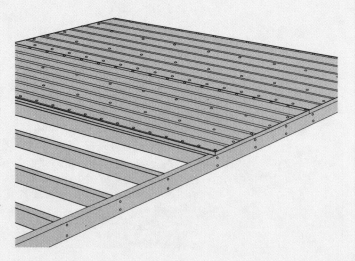

Installing the walls

TOOLKIT
- Claw hammer
- Carpenter's level
- Tape measure
- Wrench

1 ▶ Raising a wall

With two helpers lending a hand—one worker on each end and one in the middle—lift the first wall up so its top is about waist-high. Then, keeping the wall tilted slightly forward, slide it toward the edge of the slab until the inside edge of the sole plate lines up with the chalk line; the anchor bolts should be in line with the holes drilled in the sole plate.

Once it's in position, slowly raise the wall by "walking" your hands down the studs. Have your helpers hold the wall in place until it's braced, as described below.

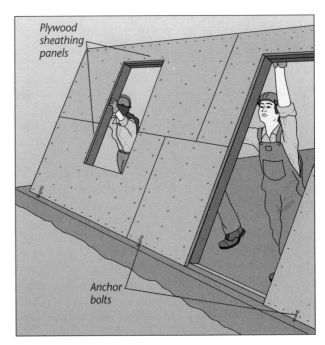

Plywood sheathing panels

Anchor bolts

1x4 brace

Block

Carpenter's level

Straight board

Block

◀ 2 Bracing and plumbing a wall

To brace the wall, tack three 1x4 braces to the wall studs—one near each end and another in the middle. Nail the lower ends of the braces to the sides of 2x4 blocks anchored to the ground with stakes. By eye, check the wall for plumb, and then nail the blocks to wooden stakes. Using a carpenter's level, check the wall for plumb along both end studs on adjacent faces. If a stud is warped, bridge the warp with a straight board with two small blocks attached so you can get a true reading for plumb. Where the wall is out of plumb, loosen that brace, align the wall, and nail the brace back in place. Once both ends are plumb, adjust the middle *(left)*.

3 Anchoring the walls

Before you anchor the first wall permanently, raise, brace, and plumb the remaining walls. Install the side (long) walls first, then add the end walls. Now measure the diagonals from corner to corner across the slab. Adjust the walls as necessary until the diagonals match. Also check the walls for level; drive cedar shingle shims under the sole plate if necessary.

When everything is aligned, use an adjustable wrench to tighten a nut onto each anchor bolt. Plumb the corners, then nail through the end walls into the corner posts in the side walls with 3" nails staggered every 12".

4 Adding interior walls and top plates

Indicate the correct layout of interior walls with a snapped chalk line. Interior walls are raised, braced, and plumbed just like exterior walls. Where they intersect exterior walls, nail through the end studs into the exterior studs with 3" nails staggered every 12". When all the walls are anchored, nail a second set of top plates—the "top cap"—onto the first, offsetting all joints below by at least 4'. At corners and intersections, overlap the joints below. Space 3½" nails every 16", and use two nails at joints and intersections. Leave all braces in place until the ceiling joists and rafters are installed.

ROOF FRAMING

Though not all roofs look alike, most configurations are variations on the basic gable roof, which consists of evenly spaced pairs of common rafters running from the top plates to a central ridgeboard at the peak.

Unless you're working with premade trusses, the framing sequence includes installing ceiling joists; measuring, cutting, and assembling rafters; and finishing with gable studs, barge rafters, and, if required, collar beams.

Trusses: These framing members are prefabricated assemblies engineered to meet the structural requirements of a particular building. The W-type truss *(below, bottom)* is one of the most common configurations. Although they're easy to work with—you order them to perfectly fit your design specifications—they take up more attic space, eliminating much of the headroom. And they're more expensive than traditional rafter framing.

To install trusses, place them upside down on the top plate of the outside walls (you'll need helpers to do this). One by one, move them into position—usually on 2-foot centers—and swing them up. The best way to do this is to have two workers on ladders at each end and one worker standing inside the structure pushing the truss up with a long pole. Toenail the trusses in place and check for plumb. (You may need to brace the end trusses with ground stakes to keep them plumb.) Fasten 1x4 lateral bracing to the top of each truss to keep them in alignment as you secure them to the top plate with framing anchors.

Rafters: Rafters are the angled framing members that form part of the sloping sides of a roof, and support the roof deck and roofing materials. They are usually 2x6s, 2x8s, or 2x10s installed on either 16- or 24-inch centers. Rafter size depends on span, spacing, and the load to be carried; your local building department will have all the variables worked out. At the peak, rafter pairs butt against a central ridgeboard—either 1-by or 2-by lumber. Choose a ridgeboard that is one width larger than the rafters; for example, if you have 2x6 rafters, use an 8-inch-wide ridgeboard. When you lay out a rafter, measure, mark, and cut one perfectly, using it as a pattern for the rest; use the "stepping off" method described beginning on page 54.

Before you cut and install the rafters, you must determine the slope, or pitch, of the roof. Although roofs with steep slopes require longer rafters and

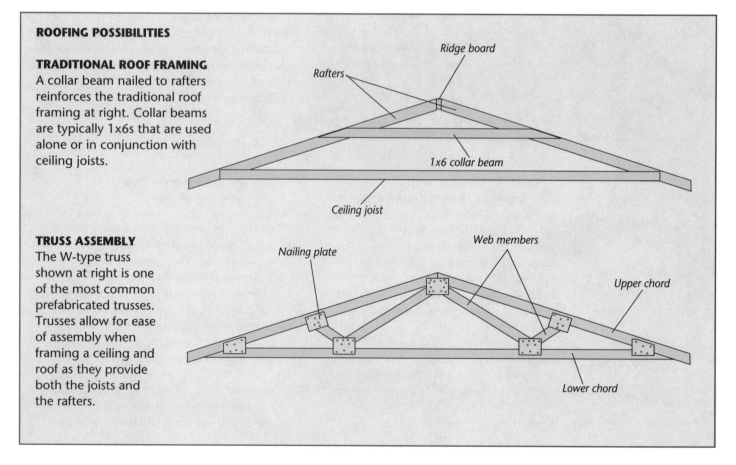

ROOFING POSSIBILITIES

TRADITIONAL ROOF FRAMING
A collar beam nailed to rafters reinforces the traditional roof framing at right. Collar beams are typically 1x6s that are used alone or in conjunction with ceiling joists.

Ridge board
Rafters
1x6 collar beam
Ceiling joist

TRUSS ASSEMBLY
The W-type truss shown at right is one of the most common prefabricated trusses. Trusses allow for ease of assembly when framing a ceiling and roof as they provide both the joists and the rafters.

Nailing plate
Web members
Upper chord
Lower chord

more building material, they also provide greater headroom in the attic and are best for "shedding" snow in colder climates. A pitch of 6 in 12 or steeper is recommended in areas with a lot of snowfall. Roofs with less of an angle are suitable in warmer climates. A pitch of 3 in 12 is usually the minimum allowed for rafter framing.

Check the walls for square once more before installing the rafters; measure diagonals from corner to corner across the top plates. Safety is the major concern when framing a roof. Always take time to plan the proper operating sequence before you start.

Joists: These horizontal framing members are placed on edge and nailed to the walls' top plate *(below, right)*. They support the load of the ceiling materials below, and help to permanently brace shed and garage walls against the thrust of the rafters above. Joists normally span the structure's width, resting on opposite walls; they may also rest on a beam or bearing wall at the center.

As with rafters, joists are typically made of 2x6, 2x8, or 2x10 lumber, and are spaced 16 or 24 inches on center. Because the ceiling of one level may become the floor of the next, you'll want to plan for the floor as well, and space the joists accordingly. When a floor is in the plans, joists are typically spaced 16 inches on center. If you don't plan to use the attic space in your garage, the joists may be spaced as far as 4 feet apart.

Joist size depends on several factors including lumber species and grade, total span, the type of ceiling below, and the amount of traffic or storage space needed in the attic above. Consult your local building code's span charts before planning joist locations.

It's possible that your shed or garage may be designed to include collar beams instead of joists, or in conjunction with joists spaced farther apart. Collar beams provide added support and, if used instead of joists, offer a feeling of openness to the finished interior.

Installing ceiling joists

TOOLKIT
- Tape measure
- Combination square or framing square
- Circular saw
- Claw hammer

1 ▶ Laying out the joists
The positions of ceiling joists are laid out along the top plates with a tape measure and combination square or with a 16" long framing square. It's safest to stand on a firm ladder while you mark the spacings. Lay the rafters out at the same time; if their spacings are the same, place rafters and joists next to one another, so that when the rafters are installed, they can be nailed to the joists. If spacings are different—24" and 16" O.C.—space them so they'll meet every 48". Many carpenters position a joist just inside the top plate on each end wall to provide a solid nailing base for ceiling materials at the edge. Plan to butt long spans together, as shown in step 2.

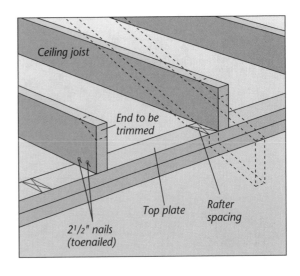

2 ◀ Installing the joists
Cut all the joists to length, then pull them up into position and nail them down. This takes two carpenters working from ladders at opposite ends. Toenail the joists to each plate with three 2¹/₂" nails. If the joists butt together at the center, nail each to the plate or beam and tie them together with 2-by blocking *(left)*.

When a partition wall's top plate falls between parallel joists, install nailing blocks every 2' and toenail through the blocks into the plate. Frame a ceiling opening in the same manner as you would a floor opening *(page 100)*.

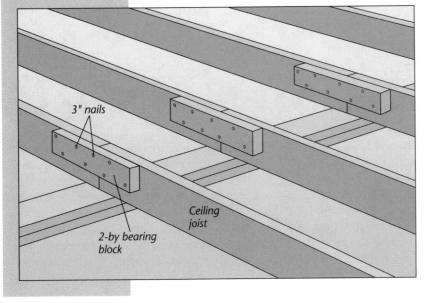

Basic roofing terms that you'll need to understand include span, run, and rise *(below)*. Note that the outline of the run, the rise, and a rafter's top edge form a right-angled triangle. Then remember the Pythagorean theorem for right-angled triangles: $A^2 + B^2 = C^2$. If run and rise—A and B below—are known, then the length of C—the rafter—can

be quickly calculated. The slope (pitch) of a roof is usually simplified in terms of unit rise and unit run. Unit run is always 12 inches; unit rise equals slope in those 12 inches. You may hear a roof described as—for example—"5 in 12." This means that the roof rises 5 inches vertically for every 12 inches of run.

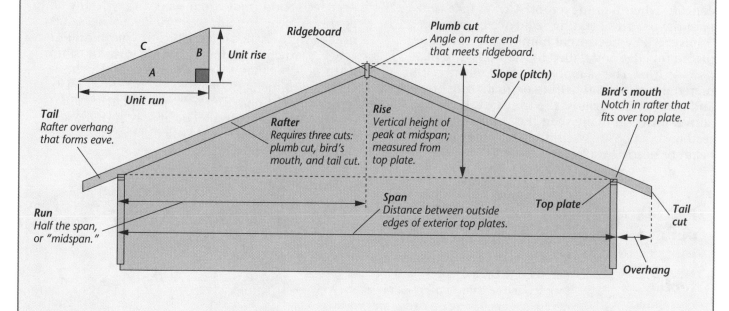

Ridgeboard

Plumb cut
Angle on rafter end that meets ridgeboard.

Unit rise

Unit run

Slope (pitch)

Bird's mouth
Notch in rafter that fits over top plate.

Tail
Rafter overhang that forms eave.

Rafter
Requires three cuts: plumb cut, bird's mouth, and tail cut.

Rise
Vertical height of peak at midspan; measured from top plate.

Span
Distance between outside edges of exterior top plates.

Top plate

Tail cut

Run
Half the span, or "midspan."

Overhang

Laying out a rafter by stepping off

TOOLKIT
• Framing square
• Square gauges (optional)

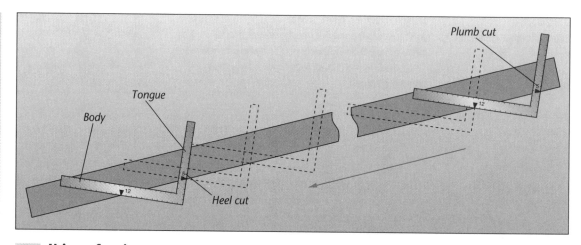

Plumb cut

Tongue

Body

Heel cut

1 Using a framing square

To "step off" a rafter, choose a straight piece of lumber for your pattern; if there's a crown (the higher edge of a warped rafter), place the crown side away from you (the rafters will be installed crown-side up). Now, align the framing square so that the figure for unit run—12—and the figure representing unit rise (5 in the example above) on the outside of the body and tongue, respectively, meet the rafter's edge. To mark the plumb cut, trace a

pencil line along the tongue. Then draw a line along the body. Move the framing square down the rafter until the 5 figure on the tongue intersects the line you drew along the body at the rafter edge; line up the 12 figure with the rafter's edge again and draw another line along the body. Continue stepping off increments in the same way. If you're measuring a run of 10', for instance, step off 10 times. Square gauges are useful for this task.

2 Marking the bird's mouth

Align the square again and draw a new line along the tongue; this line is the heel cut of the bird's mouth. To lay out the horizontal seat cut of the bird's mouth, measure up 1½" from the bottom end of the heel line. Slide the square back toward the top of the rafter, keeping the figures lined up, until the edge of the body intersects the 1½" mark (below). Draw the seat cut line along the body. If your actual run is an odd increment like 10'8", extend the line along the body on your 10th step with the square, then make a mark at 20"—8 extra inches. Slide the square down the rafter until the tongue aligns with this mark; draw a heel cut. For an overhang, step the overhang off from the heel cut. The rafter tail can be cut plumb, level, or perpendicular to the rafter.

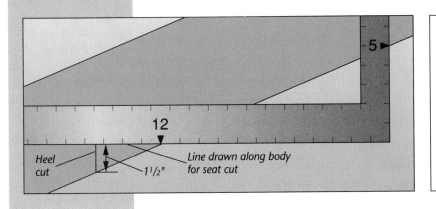

Heel cut

1½"

12

Line drawn along body for seat cut

5 ▶

3 Accounting for the ridgeboard

The total rafter distance you have laid out represents the theoretical length—just as if there were no ridgeboard at the peak. You must now go back and subtract one-half of the thickness of the ridgeboard—³/₈" for a 1-by ridgeboard, ³/₄" for a 2-by ridgeboard—and then draw a parallel line inside the original plumb cut line.

ASK A PRO

HOW DO I USE THE TABLES ON MY FRAMING SQUARE?

Below each inch mark on the body's face side is a column of six or seven figures. The inch marks on the body serve as an index to unit rise; in our example, we'd check the column under the 5-inch figure. The top set of numbers represents the "length common rafters per foot run." Thus, for every 12 inches of unit run and 5 inches of rise, the rafter length will be 13 inches. Multiplying this by the 10 feet of run in our example gives you 130 inches—or 10 feet, 10 inches.

(NOTE: The charts on your square may differ from those discussed; consult the instruction booklet.)

To lay out the rafter, draw the plumb cut at the top by aligning the square as described in step 1. Now measure the actual distance (10 feet, 10 inches) along the rafter edge to the heel cut. Lay out the heel and seat cuts, as described earlier, and add on the tail's length. Subtract half the thickness of the ridgeboard from the theoretical length you've laid out.

Assembling a gable roof

TOOLKIT
- Circular saw
- Crosscut saw
- Chisel (optional)
- Tape measure
- Claw hammer
- Carpenter's level
- Plumb bob

1 Making the cuts

Although plumb and tail cuts are straightforward, a bird's mouth requires special care. Beginning with a circular saw, cut along the heel and seat cut lines only to the point where they intersect. Finish the corner with a crosscut saw held upright. If a rough edge remains, clean it out with a sharp chisel.

2 Preparing the rafters and ridgeboard

After your first rafter is laid out and cut, make a duplicate so you'll have a pair. To check your work, get some helpers and place the rafters up on the ceiling joists. For solid footing, tack plywood sheets on the joists. Attach a scrap block of the same material you'll use for the ridgeboard to one rafter's plumb cut. Then raise both rafters into position; they should be snug against the top plate at both ends and flush with the ridgeboard scrap. If so, take them down and cut the remaining rafters.

Measure and cut the ridgeboard to length, transferring the rafter spacing marks to its sides. If your structure is too long for a single ridgeboard, the joint should fall between a rafter pair. For a gable overhang (rake), the ridgeboard must extend the appropriate distance beyond the end rafters.

3 Installing the end rafters

To begin raising a garage or shed roof, nail two upright 2x4 braces flush against the wall's top plate, as shown below. Prop each rafter against the top plate near its intended mark; when you need a rafter, pull it up into position. Align the first end rafter flush with the end wall's top plate. It takes two peo- ple to raise a large rafter: The first lines the rafter up with the end of the plate; the second raises it into position, making sure the bird's mouth is snug on the top plate, and then toenail the rafter to the plate with three 2½" nails, or with a metal framing connector. Finally, tack the rafter to the 2x4 brace.

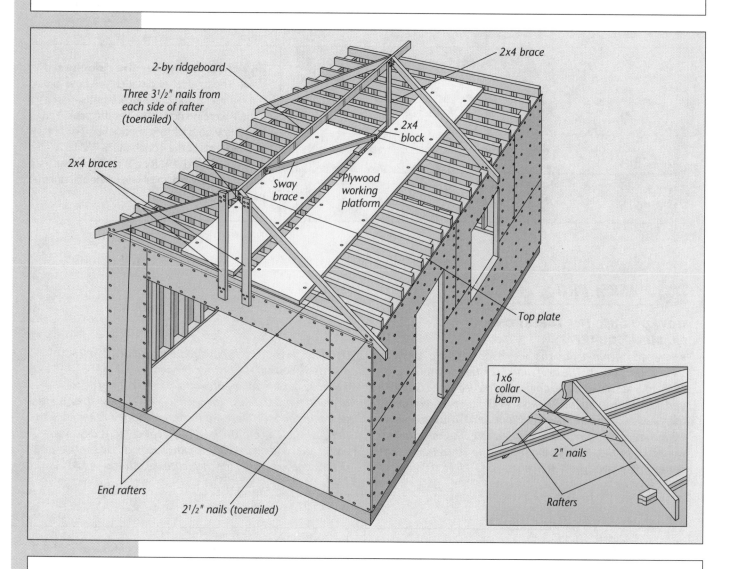

2-by ridgeboard

Three 3½" nails from each side of rafter (toenailed)

2x4 braces

2x4 brace

2x4 block

Sway brace

Plywood working platform

Top plate

End rafters

2½" nails (toenailed)

1x6 collar beam

2" nails

Rafters

4 Raising and bracing the ridgeboard

With a helper, raise the ridgeboard into position, align it with the top of the first rafter, and nail it to the rafter with three nails: 2½" for a 1-by ridgeboard, or 3½" for a 2-by. If the ridgeboard is a single piece, repeat the procedure at the other gable end. If it's in two pieces, brace it at the far end, so the ridge is level; then attach one rafter at the first spacing back from the end. Now go back and install the matching rafters, toenailing them to the ridgeboard from the opposite side. The end rafters should be flush with the end of the wall, and the ridgeboard must be both level and centered over the midspan—check with a carpenter's level and plumb bob.

To brace the ridgeboard, nail a sway brace running diago- nally from the ridgeboard to a 2x4 block nailed across the joists. Add the other rafters to the run in pairs, fastening each to the top plate and then to the ridgeboard. To add a second ridgeboard, proceed as before from the other direction; the boards' junction must be covered by two rafters.

Where rafters meet ceiling joists, tie them together with three 3" nails; cut the joist ends to match the rafter slope.

Long spans can be tied together with collar beams or ties (inset). The number of collar beams you need (one per pair of rafters or only every other pair) is specified in your plan.

Filling in gable ends; framing overhangs

TOOLKIT
- Tape measure
- Carpenter's level
- T-bevel
- Circular saw
- Claw hammer
- Chalk line

1 Adding gable studs

With the rafters in place, start at the point directly below the peak, centering a stud on this spot. Now move toward both ends of the plate, laying out stud spacings on 16" centers. The first stud fits securely between the ridgeboard and top plate. To lay out the remaining studs, position one on its mark, flush against the end rafter, and check it for plumb. Trace the rafter angle onto the edge of the stud. Then mark an adjacent stud.

The difference in length between these studs is called the common difference, and will be consistent between each adjacent stud in the row. Cut the studs in pairs at the correct angle, using a T-bevel to transfer the angle. Notch the studs to fit over the joist. Toenail each stud to the plate and rafter with 3" nails. If your plans call for a gable end vent, frame the opening with horizontal 2x4s bridging the studs.

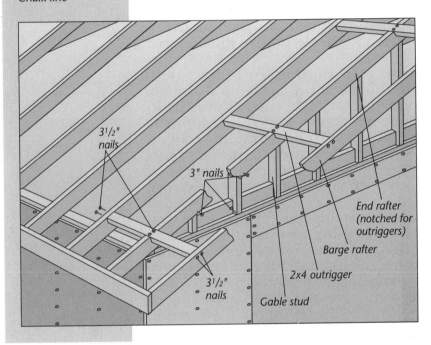

3½" nails

3" nails

End rafter (notched for outriggers)

Barge rafter

2x4 outrigger

3½" nails

Gable stud

2 Adding outriggers

To form a roof overhang at the gable end (rake), add outriggers and a pair of barge rafters to the ridgeboard extending past the end walls. Outriggers are 2x4s laid flat and positioned perpendicular to the rafters. Spaced every 4' down from the ridgeboard, they begin at the first rafters in from the end rafters; end rafters are notched so that the outriggers sit flush with the roof plane. Nail outriggers to the first pair of rafters and then into end rafters at notches, using 3½" nails. Leave them slightly longer than the ridgeboard; snap a chalk line 1½" in from the end of the ridgeboard and cut the outriggers off. Position barge rafters as shown at left, nailing them to the ridgeboard and into the ends of the outriggers. NOTE: Exercise caution—the gable overhang is the most dangerous area to work on the entire roof.

COMMON ROOF SHAPES

Whether you're installing a roof on a shed or a garage, there are several styles to choose from. In this section, we've shown you framing for gable roofs (below, left), but gambrel roofs (below, middle) and shed roofs (below, right) are also popular. A gambrel roof resembles the roof of a barn. Typically, it has two pitches, at 30° and 60° from horizontal. In shed roof construction, one wall is made shorter than the other to create a roof with a single sloping plane.

Gable roof

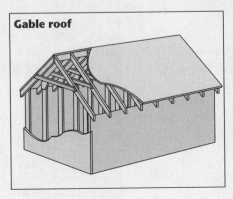

Gambrel roof

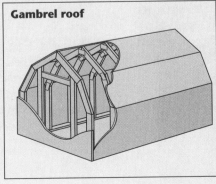

Shed roof

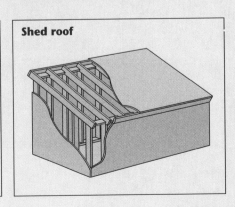

FINISHING THE EXTERIOR

After your shed or garage has been framed, the next step is to finish the exterior. Doing a good job at this stage is crucial for two reasons: First, and most importantly, you'll want to protect the structure from the weather as best you can; second, this is the point where you'll add the decorative touches that suit your taste.

This chapter begins with an overview of the exterior of a typical garage (many of the elements also apply to sheds), illustrating how the "skin" protects the structure. All of the elements shown are featured on the subsequent pages, starting with preparing the roof on page 60, and finishing it with asphalt shingles *(page 62)*. To install a gutter system on the edge of your roof, turn to page 75. Both open and closed soffits are shown on page 73.

Once the roof is in place, it's time to add doors and windows. Details for installing two styles of prehung windows and a prehung door are featured in the section beginning on page 64. Instructions for adding a garage door with an automatic opener begin on page 77.

The addition of siding, secured to the sheathing of the structure, is the final step in finishing the exterior. Preparing the walls for the siding, as well as examples of two types of finish—solid board and plywood—are covered beginning on page 68. Tips for painting or staining the siding are given on page 74.

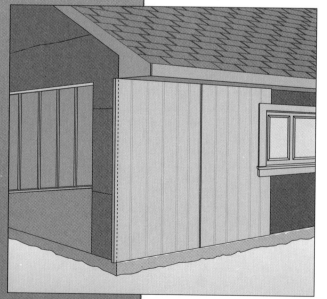

With the roof finished, the next stage is adding windows and doors. Plywood siding may be applied over sheathing and building paper to finish the walls. Turn to page 71 for details.

APPLYING THE SKIN

There are many different elements that comprise the exterior envelope, or "skin," of a structure. Shown below is a view of a typical garage with each vital component highlighted.

Beginning on the roof, the sheathing forms the base (often called the "roof deck") for the finish roofing material. Depending on the type of roofing, sheathing can be plywood, as shown, lumber, or open, spaced boards. The fascia is comprised of boards attached to the rafter ends at the eaves and along the gables. A drip edge prevents water from getting under the roofing material. Roofing felt laid on top of the sheathing acts as a barrier between the roof deck and the roofing material. Asphalt shingles are a common finish for garages and sheds; they'll last between 12 and 40 years, depending on quality.

The plywood sheathing applied to the framing of the walls helps strengthen the overall structure and serves as a solid nailing base for the siding. The building paper is usually tacked over the sheathing to provide a barrier against wind and water. It must be attached before the siding is installed.

The solid board siding shown is typical of garages; sheet materials, masonry, metal, or vinyl siding can also be used. Wood trim, or casing, provides the finish between the siding and the frames of the doors and windows as well as at the corners of the garage.

The garage door will either be wood, aluminum, steel, or fiberglass. The doors are often insulated with a poly core. It's important to install weather stripping around the exterior perimeter of the door to keep the wind and the rain out of the garage.

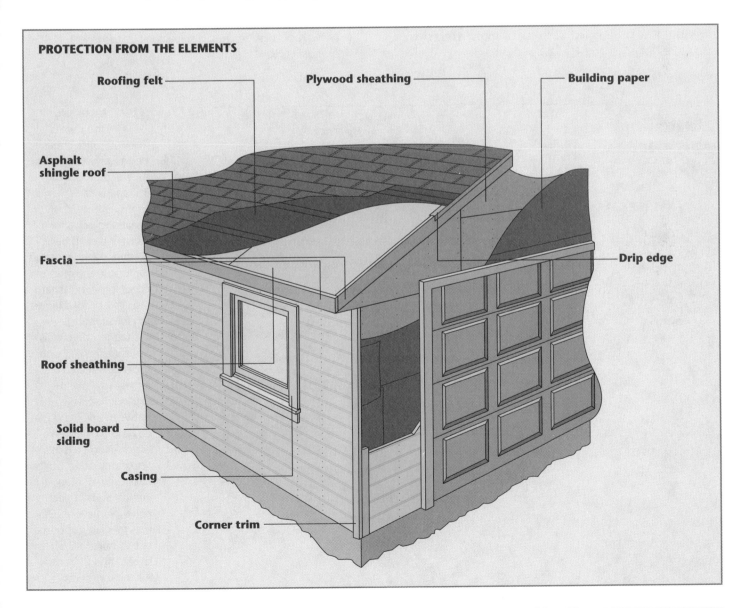

PROTECTION FROM THE ELEMENTS

- Roofing felt
- Plywood sheathing
- Building paper
- Asphalt shingle roof
- Drip edge
- Fascia
- Roof sheathing
- Solid board siding
- Casing
- Corner trim

ROOFING

Once the frame is finished, it is time to add the roof. In this section we show you how to install asphalt shingles. This is an easy and relatively inexpensive way of surfacing the roof of your garage or shed. Other options you could consider include slate, wooden shakes or shingles, or aluminum or steel panels. Ideally, your choice of material and installation pattern should harmonize with the roof of your house.

PREPARING THE ROOF

Asphalt shingles go over a solid deck of plywood sheathing, with an underlayment of 15-pound roofing felt. Flashing protects your roof at vulnerable points—valleys, vents, chimneys, skylights, and eaves— anywhere water can seep through. It's usually made of malleable 28-gauge galvanized sheet metal. On asphalt shingle roofs, valleys and vents may also be flashed with mineral-surface roll roofing. Plastics or aluminum are used too, and copper may be preferred for chimney flashing. Buy preformed flashing or make your own.

Installing plywood decking and underlayment

TOOLKIT
- Claw hammer
- Tape measure
- Chalk line
For underlayment:
- Utility knife
- Staple gun (optional)

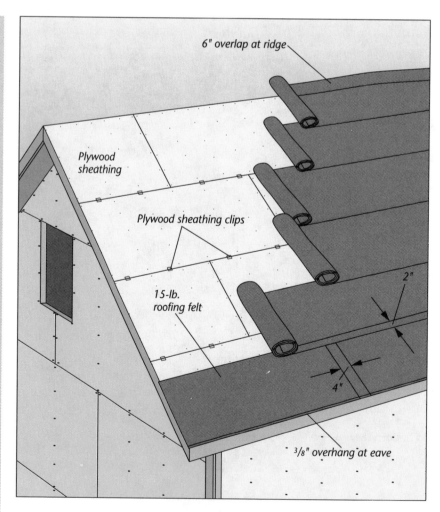

6" overlap at ridge

Plywood sheathing

Plywood sheathing clips

15-lb. roofing felt

2"

4"

3/8" overhang at eave

1 Installing the sheets
Though some codes permit plywood as thin as 5/16" on roofs with 16" spans, or 3/8" on 24" spans, either 1/2" or 5/8" sheathing will offer a sturdier nailing base. (Lighter panels may call for tongue-and-groove edges, plywood sheathing clips, or solid blocking for support.)

Stagger the panels horizontally (*left*), with the ends centered on rafters. To allow for expansion, leave 1/16" between adjoining panels, and 1/8" between edges (double this in a very humid area). Space nails every 6" along the vertical ends of each panel, and every 12" at intermediate supports. Use 2" nails for 1/2" sheets, and 2 1/2" nails for thicker sheets.

2 Rolling out the underlayment

To align rows of underlayment evenly, measure the roof carefully and, if underlayment is not premarked, snap horizontal chalk lines before you begin. Snap the first line 33⅝" above the eave (this allows for a ⅜" overhang). Then, providing for a 2" overlap between strips of felt, snap each succeeding chalk line at 34". To apply the felt, start at the eave and lay the strips horizontally along the roof, working toward the ridge. Felt should be trimmed flush at the rake (gable end) and overlapped 6" at any valleys, hips, and ridges. Where two strips meet in a vertical line, overlap them by 4". Drive just enough staples or nails to hold the felt in place (generally, one for every square yard of felt).

Installing valley flashing

TOOLKIT
- Tape measure
- Claw hammer
- Tin snips

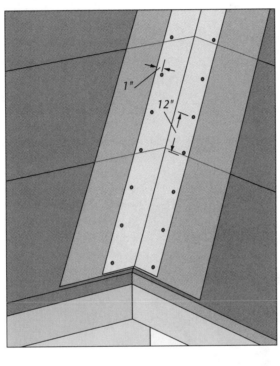

Laying the flashings

Valleys require particularly sturdy flashing because they carry more water off a roof than does any individual roof plane. To install the flashing, first roll out a length of 15-pound roofing felt cut to the length of the valley. Push it snugly into the valley, and, using roofing nails, nail it every 2' to 4' along the outside edges. If you'll need more than one length of flashing to cover the valley, start at the bottom and let the top piece overlap the bottom one by at least 6". Nail every 12" along the flashings' edges. Use roofing nails of the same metal as the flashing; two different metals can interact to cause oxidation. At ridges or where two valleys meet, cut flashings with tin snips so you can overlap them (the upper one over the lower) and nail them down.

Installing drip edge

TOOLKIT
- Claw hammer
- Tin snips

Protecting the eaves

Drip edges keep water from wicking back under the roofing material along eaves and rakes. Along the eaves, the drip edge goes under the roofing felt; at the rake, the drip edge goes on top of the felt.

Fit the drip edge for the eaves tightly against the fascia board (if there is one) and nail through the top deck surface (not the fascia) at about 10" intervals, using roofing nails. Overlap adjoining lengths about 1"; cut them flush at the rakes. After applying the roofing felt, nail drip edges along the rakes using the same technique.

In climates where ice dams may occur along eaves, flash with a special rubber or plastic ice-shield membrane or roll roofing from the eaves to at least 12" beyond the inside wall line.

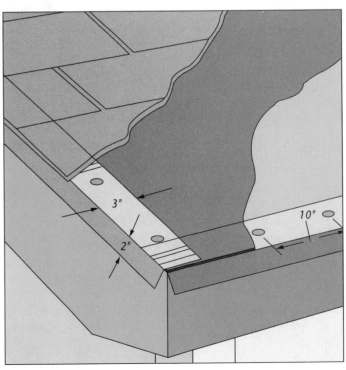

APPLYING ASPHALT SHINGLES

Asphalt shingles come in a wide variety of colors, and most have self-sealing mastic that welds one shingle tab to another by the heat of the sun after the shingles are installed. The standard asphalt shingle is 12 by 36 inches with three integral tabs *(right)*. After overlapping courses are applied, the lower 5 inches of each shingle will generally be exposed to the weather. A narrow starter row runs the length of the eave to form a base for the first full course of shingles. The instructions presented here represent a typical installation; follow the package directions for the shingles that you buy.

Cutting: To cut individual shingles, turn them over, score them with a knife, and bend them back and forth until they break off along the scored line.

Nailing: Use 12-gauge galvanized roofing nails, 1¼-inch-long with ⅜-inch-diameter heads.

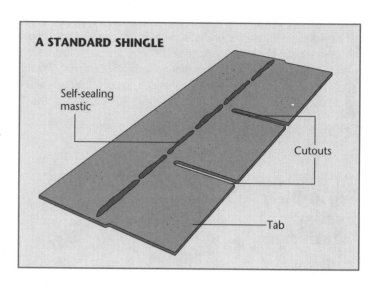

A STANDARD SHINGLE

Self-sealing mastic

Cutouts

Tab

Laying the starter course and first course

TOOLKIT
- Tape measure
- Utility knife
- Carpenter's square or straightedge
- Claw hammer

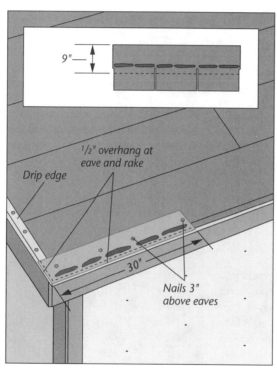

9"

½" overhang at eave and rake

Drip edge

30"

Nails 3" above eaves

Laying the starter course

To start a new roof use a 7" strip of asphalt roll roofing, or cut 3" off the tabs of the 12" wide shingles *(inset)*. Install the starter course along the eave, starting at the left rake. Shorten the first shingle by 6" to offset the cutouts. To cut shingles, use a utility knife fitted with a special hooked blade.

Allowing a ½" overhang at both eave and rake, and 1/16" spacing between shingles, fasten the shingles to the deck 3" above the eave, hammering a nail 1" from each end and 12" in from each end *(left)*.

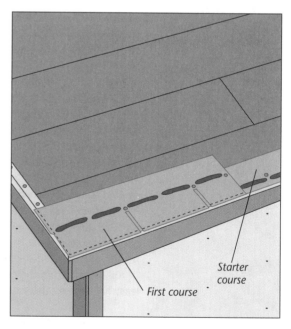

Starter course

First course

Laying the first course

Allowing the same ½" overhang at the rake and eave, and 1/16" between shingles, offset the tabs of the first course shingles by 6", then nail them over the starter course, using 4 nails per shingle *(right)*. Space these nails 5⅝" above the butt line, 1" and 12" in from each end or as directed by the manufacturer.

Laying successive courses

TOOLKIT
- Chalk line
- Tape measure
- Claw hammer
- Utility knife

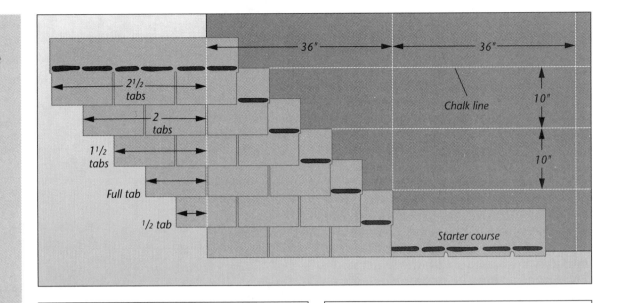

36"   36"

2½ tabs

2 tabs

1½ tabs

Full tab

½ tab

Chalk line

10"

10"

Starter course

1 Aligning the shingles
Your main concern when you lay the second and successive courses is proper alignment of the shingles—both horizontal and vertical. Aligning shingles horizontally is simply a matter of snapping chalk lines across the roof deck. Snap lines every 10" from the bottom of the first course, as shown above. Then, as you move toward the ridge, make sure that the upper edge of every other course of shingles lines up against the chalk lines. Before you start your second row of shingles, also snap vertical chalk lines from the roof ridge to one end of every shingle along the first course.

2 Installing the shingles
With standard three-tab shingles, you can produce different patterns by adjusting the length of the first shingle of each course. Centered alignment, shown above, is the most common and offers the most uniform appearance. Cutouts or shingle edges must line up—within ¼"—with cutouts or edges two rows above and below. Line up each successive row staggered by half a tab to the left. Lay each shingle just below the cutout line of the previous one. Mark the end shingle, allowing for overhang; then remove and trim it (save the pieces for the other edge of the roof). Replace the end shingle and nail the row, using the vertical chalk lines to ensure that every seventh row lines up with the first.

Installing hip and ridge shingles

TOOLKIT
- Utility knife
- Chalk line
- Tape measure
- Claw hammer

Cutting and applying shingles
Use ready-made ridge and hip shingles or cut 12" squares from standard shingles. Bend each; if cold, warm them first. Snap a chalk line the length of the ridge, 6" from the center. Starting at the end opposite the prevailing wind, apply the shingles with a 5" exposure. Each edge should line up with a chalk mark. Nail on each side, 5½" from the butt and 1" from outside edge (inset). For a hip roof (right), shingle each hip in the same way. Start with a double layer at the bottom of the hip and work toward the ridge. Use nails about 2" long. Dab the exposed nailheads of the last shingle with plastic roofing cement.

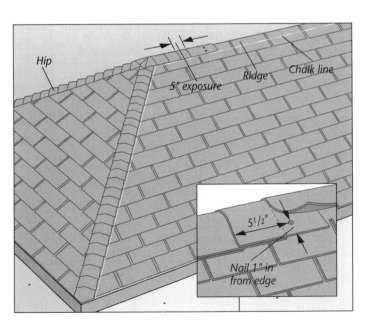

Hip

5" exposure

Ridge

Chalk line

5½"

Nail 1" in from edge

WINDOWS AND DOORS

The most popular styles of windows are double-hung, sliding, casement, and fixed. The most widely used, double-hung windows, have an upper, outside sash that moves down, and a lower, inside sash that moves up in grooves in the frame. Sliding windows have movable sashes that slide in horizontal tracks. Casement windows, hung singly or in pairs, have sashes that swing outward; the modern ones are operated with a crank. Fixed windows, often called "picture" windows, are stationary units mounted within a frame.

In general, wooden windows (page 65) are attached to the sheathing by nailing through the exterior casing, or brickmold, on the outside, and through the jambs on the inside. For aluminum, clad, or vinyl windows (page 66) nail through the factory-installed nailing strip on the outside perimeter of the window. NOTE: With some of these windows, you may have to nail through the jambs. Always follow the manufacturer's installation instructions.

Modern manufactured doors come in two types: panel and flush. Panel doors, as shown at right, consist of solid vertical stiles and horizontal rails, with filler panels between. Superior strength and good looks make this style a wise choice for exterior doors. Your dealer may also have the newer composite or steel doors.

Installing a door in the traditional way means constructing a door frame, positioning it in the rough door opening, hinging the door to the frame, and installing a latch or lockset. If you buy a prehung door, much of the work has been done for you: the door comes hinged to the jamb, and frequently casing, lock, latch, and strike plate are included, too. Installation consists of centering the frame and then leveling and plumbing it (page 66) within the rough opening created when you build the walls (page 48).

A typical height for exterior doors is 6 feet 10 inches. Width and thickness vary; choose a width from 32 to 36 inches, and a thickness of 1³/₄ inches.

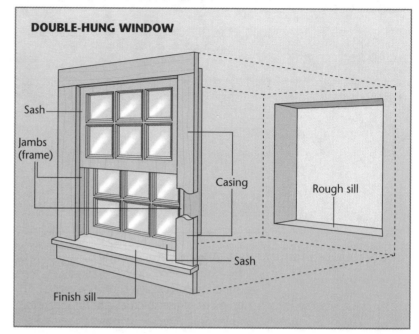

DOUBLE-HUNG WINDOW

Sash · Jambs (frame) · Casing · Rough sill · Sash · Finish sill

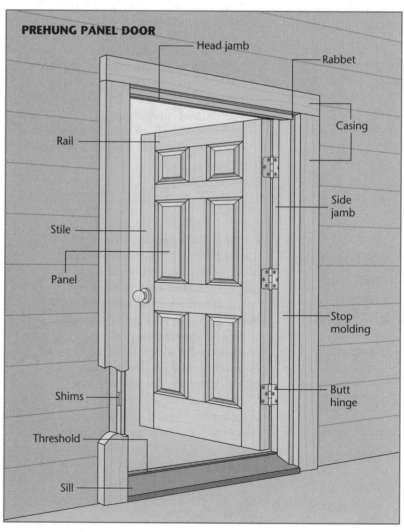

PREHUNG PANEL DOOR

Head jamb · Rabbet · Casing · Rail · Stile · Panel · Side jamb · Stop molding · Shims · Butt hinge · Threshold · Sill

Installing a prehung wooden window

TOOLKIT
- Carpenter's level
- Hand stapler (optional)
- Carpenter's square
- Claw hammer
- Electric drill
- Caulking gun
- Crosscut saw
- Nailset

Carpenter's level

1 Leveling the window

From outside the building, center the window in the opening and have a helper hold it in place. While one person checks for plumb with a carpenter's level (left), the other person should be inside placing shims between the bottom jamb and the rough sill, until the window is level.

To help keep out the weather, fiberglass-reinforced flashing paper is recommended. It comes in rolls about 8" wide, and is installed on all sides of the window. Place it on top of the sheathing but under the brickmold. The bottom piece goes on first, then the side pieces, overlapping the bottom, and finally the top piece, which overlaps the sides. Hold it in place with a few staples, near the outside edge of each strip, where they'll be covered by the siding.

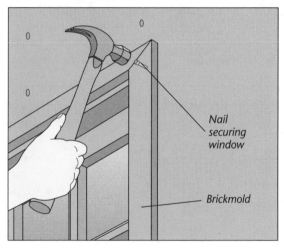

Nail securing window

Brickmold

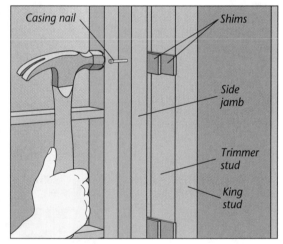

Casing nail

Shims

Side jamb

Trimmer stud

King stud

2 Fastening the window

With the window centered, drive a 3¼-inch galvanized finishing nail through one corner of the exterior casing, or brickmold (above, left). Check the window for level. If it is, nail the other corners. If it isn't, have your helper adjust the shims before nailing the remaining corners. The shims should be spaced about 12" apart; make sure they are not so tight that they push the jamb out of plumb (check with a carpenter's square). Once all the corners have been nailed, nail every 12" along the exterior casing, countersinking the nails and filling the holes with wood putty.

With the window secured on the outside, go inside the building and nail through the jambs and each set of shims to the trimmer stud, using 2½" casing nails (above, right); drill pilot holes for the nails first. Saw or break off the shims flush with the jambs.

Unless your roof has a pronounced overhang, it's a good idea to install flashing, also known as a drip cap, over the top of the window. After you've applied the siding (page 68), thoroughly caulk the gap between the siding and the window to weatherproof it.

Installing a window equipped with a nailing flange

TOOLKIT
- Carpenter's level
- Claw hammer
- Caulking gun

Mounting the window

Aluminum, vinyl, or clad windows have a factory-installed nailing flange, as shown at right, to secure the window in place.

As with wooden windows, center the unit in the opening and make sure it's level. Then nail the window to the sheathing through the nailing holes in the flange using 1" roofing nails. The finished siding will butt up against the outside of the window, concealing the flange. Apply a bead of caulking all around the window to weatherproof it.

For this type of window, the flashing paper goes under the nailing flange at the bottom, but on top of the flange at the sides and top.

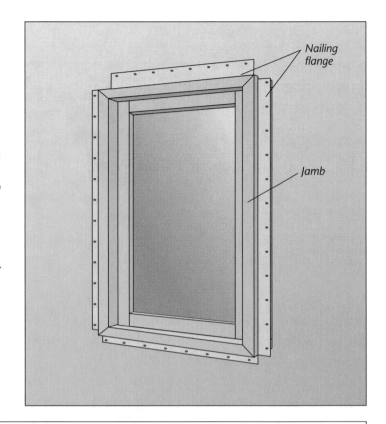

Nailing flange

Jamb

Installing a prehung door

TOOLKIT
- Carpenter's level
- Handsaw
- Claw hammer
For lockset:
- Electric drill with spade bit and hole saw
- Chisel or router with straight bit and hinge template
- Screwdriver

1 **Centering the door frame**
Exterior doors need a sill sloping to the outside and a threshold at the jambs' base. Remove the sole plate between trimmer studs (*page 48*). Fit the jamb assembly into the opening. Shim until the head jamb is the correct height and level. Center the frame in the rough opening so that an equal amount extends past each side. The interior and exterior wall coverings (wallboard, sheathing, and siding) will butt against it.

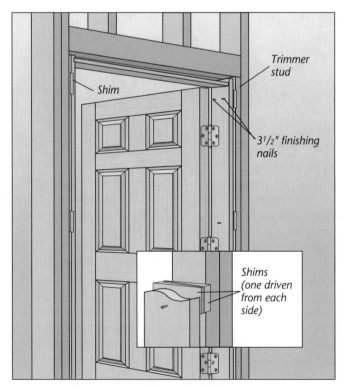

Shim

Trimmer stud

3½" finishing nails

Shims (one driven from each side)

2 **Leveling and plumbing a door frame**
Beginning next to the lower hinge location, drive two shims snugly between the side jamb and trimmer stud—one from each side (*inset*). Nail through the jamb and shims partway into the stud with a 3½" finishing nail; position the nail where the stop molding will cover it. Insert shims next to the upper hinge location, check the jamb for plumb, and nail partway. Again, shim, plumb, and nail halfway between the top and middle hinge positions. Repeat between the middle and bottom hinges. Now shim the opposite jamb at similar locations, but don't nail where you'll need to cut for the latch. Check the frame once more for plumb. Drive the nails home and set the heads with a nailset. Nail the threshold between the jambs.

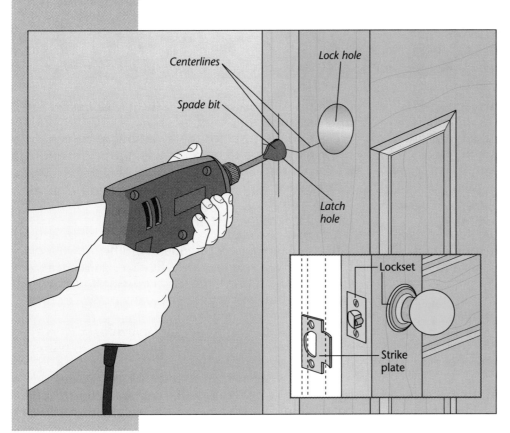

Centerlines

Spade bit

Lock hole

Latch hole

Lockset

Strike plate

3 Installing the lockset

If the holes for the lockset aren't already bored, a template and instructions for doing so should be included with your lockset. Place the knob 36" to 38" above the floor. Bore the holes using an electric drill with a spade bit and hole saw; always drill the lock hole first. When drilling the latch hole *(left)*, make sure that the drill bit remains perpendicular to the edge of the door. Next, close the door and mark the top and bottom of the latch where it contacts the jamb. Position the strike plate there; rout or chisel out a mortise for the latch, then screw the strike plate *(inset)* to the jamb.

A RAMP FOR EASY ACCESS

A simple ramp can make access into sheds and garages much easier. With a ramp, you won't have to struggle to lift items like wheelbarrows or lawn mowers inside.

The ramp should be wide enough to accommodate the equipment you want to move (about 3 feet is sufficient). The stringers can be made of pressure-treated 2-by lumber. For ramps more than 3 feet wide, add another stringer in the middle. Nail 2x4s or 2x6s across the middle.

For extra security, add a kicker plate and fasten it with anchor bolts to a concrete pad under the ramp.

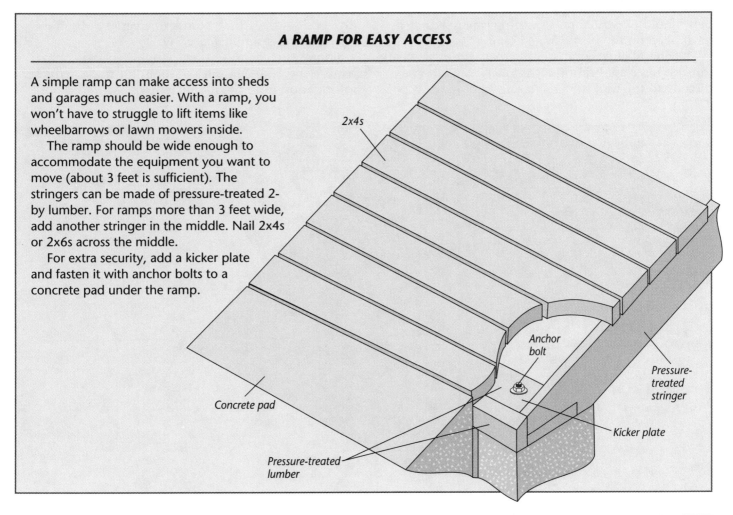

2x4s

Anchor bolt

Pressure-treated stringer

Concrete pad

Kicker plate

Pressure-treated lumber

SIDING

Where the protection of your garage or shed is concerned, siding is every bit as important as a good roof. But siding offers more than protection. The color, texture, and pattern create the "look" your structure presents to the world, so you'll want to pick a material that wears well from an esthetic, as well as a practical point of view. In most cases, a garage is sided with the same material as the house.

Sheathing is used under some siding materials for a variety of purposes: to increase their rigidity, help brace the structure, serve as a solid base for nailing, and improve insulation. Plywood is a popular choice because the large panels are easy to apply and usually afford enough lateral strength to eliminate the need for bracing during the framing of a structure. Check your local building code to determine whether structural sheathing is required with the type of siding that you've chosen.

Rigid foam insulation boards come in 4x8, 4x4, or 2x8 panels. Some types can double as nonstructural exterior sheathing for light frame construction with corner bracing. (When nailing them in place, use washers to avoid tearing the foam and to provide a better hold). If structural sheathing is required, it can be applied on top of the foam boards.

The chart below compares the main types of sheathing and basic application techniques. Nail all types directly to the wall studs. As a rule, choose rustproof common nails that will penetrate at least one inch into the studs.

Once you've installed the sheathing, some local codes require you to install building paper, a wind and water-resistant material (usually felt or kraft paper impregnated with asphalt). It comes in rolls 36 to 40 inches wide, long enough to cover 200 to 500 square feet—allowing for overlap.

You may also want to choose building paper if your siding will be subjected frequently to heavy winds or to wind-driven rain or snow. It's also a good idea to apply it if the siding to be used consists of narrow boards or shingles that present many places for the wind and water to penetrate.

A newer option is housewrap, a material that is wrapped around the frame of the building to prevent drafts and water penetration.

Finally comes the part that shows: the siding. This section shows how to install a common choice: solid board siding material (page 69). Two other commonly used options—hardboard and plywood lap boards—are installed in a similar manner.

Some siding also does double duty as the sheathing. Plywood siding, which comes in a variety of surface styles, is one example (page 71).

Sidings such as aluminum, vinyl, steel, and stucco require special techniques or tools; for these, request information from the manufacturer.

A COMPARISON OF WALL SHEATHINGS

Qualities	Types			
	Exterior plywood	Exterior fiberboard	Exterior gypsum board	Foam boards
Direction of application	Vertical or horizontal	Horizontal	Vertical or horizontal	Vertical
Panel sizes and types	$1/16$", $1/8$", $1/2$", or $15/32$" thickness in panels of 4'x8'; square edge.	$1/2$", $25/32$" thicknesses in 2'x8' panels; tongue-and-groove or shiplap.	$1/2$" thickness, 2'x8' panels. Tongue-and-groove.	4'x8', 4'x9'
Rigidity	Good	Fair	Good	Poor
Insulative value	Low	Good	Low	High
Nailing	Nail every 6" along panel's edge and every 12" into center supports.	Use roofing nails 3" apart along edges, 6" apart intermediately.	Drywall nails every 4" around edges and every 8" intermediately.	12" O.C. 8" O.C. around perimeter.
Diagonal bracing required on wall	No	Yes, with standard types	In some areas	Yes
General notes	Use performance-rated or exterior grade; apply panel ends spaced $1/16$" apart and edges $1/8$" apart.	Easy to handle and apply. Don't nail within $5/8$" of edges. Only a special type will serve as sole nailing base for siding.	Not a nailing base for siding.	Not structural; does not provide extra rigidity or a nailing base.

Preparing a wall for siding

TOOLKIT
- Utility knife
- Stapler (optional)
- Claw hammer
- Chalk line
- Shovel (optional)

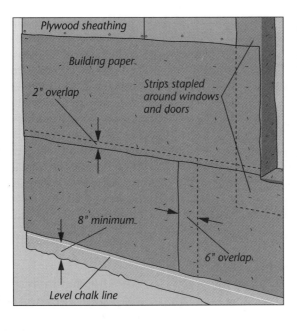

Plywood sheathing

Building paper

2" overlap

Strips stapled around windows and doors

8" minimum

6" overlap

Level chalk line

1 Applying building paper, marking the base line, and grading

Apply building paper in horizontal strips, starting at the bottom of each wall and working up, as shown at left. Overlap 2" at the horizontal joints, 6" at vertical joints; wrap the paper 12" around each corner. Cut building paper with a utility knife, and staple or nail it (with roofing nails) to studs or sheathing, using just enough fasteners to hold it in place—at a later stage, the siding nails will fasten it permanently.

For any type of siding, snap a level chalk line at least 8" above grade (ground level) to align the siding's lowest edge along the base of each wall. If necessary, excavate the surrounding soil anywhere it interferes with this 8" clearance, sloping the grade away from the structure so that water won't pool at the foundation.

INSTALLING SOLID BOARD SIDING

All solid board siding patterns can be grouped into a single category. For proper installation, however, you must treat each basic pattern individually. Consult the chart for the instructions particular to each.

Before you begin nailing up siding boards, figure out how you want to treat the corners (*page 70*). When planning your layout, try to get board rows to fall evenly around windows, doors, and other openings; with horizontal siding, a slight adjustment to the base line may do it. If you must butt board ends, stagger these joints as much as possible between successive rows.

Solid board siding needs rustproof nails. Spiral or ring-shank nails offer the best holding power. Use finishing nails if you plan to countersink and fill over nailheads.

SOLID BOARD SIDINGS			
Siding type	Direction of application	Nail size (new construction)	Nailing tips
Board on board (unmilled)	Vertical	2^1/$_2$" for under-boards; 3" for over boards	For new construction, sheathing may be required. Face-nail under boards once per bearing vertically; face-nail over boards twice, 3" to 4" apart, at center. Minimum overlap 1".
Board and batten (unmilled)	Vertical	2^1/$_2$" for under-boards; 2^1/$_2$" or 3" for battens	For new construction, sheathing may be required. Space under boards ^{1}/$_2$" apart. Face-nail boards once every 24" vertically. Minimum overlap 1".
Clapboard (unmilled)	Horizontal	3"	Face-nail 1" from overlapping edge (just above preceding course) once per bearing. Minimum overlap 1". First board requires starter strip for correct angle.
Bevel	Horizontal	2^1/$_2$" for ^{3}/$_4$" thick board; 2" for thinner board	Face-nail once per bearing, 1" from lower edge. Allow expansion clearance of ^{1}/$_8$". Minimum overlap 1". First board requires starter strip for correct angle.
Shiplap, channel rustic	Horizontal or vertical	2^1/$_2$" for 1" thick board; 2" for thinner board	For vertical application, install blocks between studs, or furring strips (on centers recommended by code). Face-nail once per bearing for 6" widths, twice (about 1" from overlapping edges) for wider styles.
Tongue-and-groove	Vertical, horizontal, or diagonal; can mix widths	2^1/$_2$" (finishing nails for blind-nailing, otherwise spiral or ring-shank nails)	For vertical or diagonal application, install blocks between studs, or furring strips (on centers recommended by code) in new construction. Blind-nail 4" to 6" widths through tongue with finishing nails, once per bearing. Face-nail wider boards with two spiral or ring-shank nails per bearing.

Installing solid board sidings

TOOLKIT
- Claw hammer
- Circular saw
- Level and plane (vertical siding)
- Combination square
- T-bevel
- Caulking gun

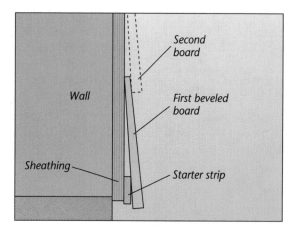

Wall

Second board

First beveled board

Sheathing

Starter strip

1 Nailing the first board
With horizontal siding, the first board goes at the bottom. Beveled and clapboard types require a starter strip beneath the board's lower edge, along the base of the wall, to push it out to match the angle of the other boards *(left)*.

For vertical wood siding, begin at one corner of the house. Align one edge of the first board with the corner and check its other edge for plumb. If it isn't plumb, adjust it as necessary; then trim the outside edge with a plane or saw until it fits the corner. Be sure the board's lower end is flush with your base line; then nail it in place.

2 Installing successive boards
To lay out horizontal board siding, you'll need a story pole. Make this from a 1x3 that's as long as the height of your tallest wall (unless that wall is more than one story). Starting at one end, mark the pole at intervals equaling the width of the siding boards, taking the overlap into account; it will indicate the bottom of each board. Holding or tacking the story pole flush with the base line, transfer the marks to each corner and to the trim at each window and door casing. Apply the siding boards from bottom to top. Unless the type of siding is overlapped or spaced, fit the boards tightly together. To match the slope of a roofline, measure the angle with a T-bevel. Transfer the angle to each board end, then cut. Where boards will be end-joined, brush a sealant on the ends before installation and be sure to make the joint square and snug. To fit shiplap or tongue-and-groove boards around windows and doors, first rip the board to the proper width. Then bevel the back edge that will butt against the frame; this will make it easier to push the board into place and will make it look like an exact fit from the outside.

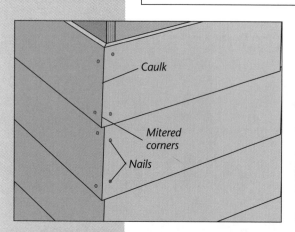

Caulk

Mitered corners

Nails

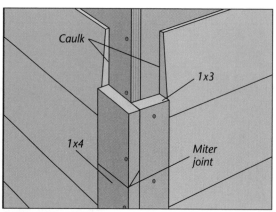

Caulk

1x3

1x4

Miter joint

2x2

Caulk

3 Covering a corner
Where siding boards meet at a corner, choose one of the three methods shown above and at left for moisture protection and a neat appearance. For an outside corner, miter the board ends *(above, left)*, or attach 1x3 and 1x4 boards to the corner for the board ends to butt against *(above, right)*. (To join these vertical boards end to end, miter the joint at a 45° angle, with the board ends sloping toward the faces as shown, to ensure proper water runoff.) A typical treatment for inside corners uses a 2x2 piece of stock for the board ends to butt against *(left)*. For any of these three corner treatments, caulk the joints.

INSTALLING PLYWOOD SIDING

There are many reasons why plywood is a popular siding material: its large panel size (4x8, 9, or 10 feet), strong laminated construction, and variety of surface styles are just a few. As well, plywood can be applied rapidly and can eliminate the need for bracing on the wall's frame.

Plywood siding applied directly to studs without sheathing must be at least $^3/_8$ inch thick for studs on 16-inch centers, and at least $^1/_2$ inch thick for studs on 24-inch centers. Panels as thin as $^5/_{16}$ inch may be applied over wall sheathing. Be sure to specify exterior-grade.

Plywood panels may be mounted either vertically or horizontally. If you choose the horizontal pattern, stag-ger vertical end joints and nail the long, horizontal edges into fire blocks or other nailing supports to make sure the joints are protected *(page 72)*. Vertical installa-tion is the most common method, since it minimizes the number of horizontal joints.

Nailing: Use rustproof nails, not finishing nails. Nails should be long enough to penetrate studs or other back-ing by $1^1/_2$ inches. For siding nailed directly to studs, use 2-inch nails for $^3/_8$-inch or $^1/_2$-inch panels, and $2^1/_2$-inch nails for $^5/_8$-inch panels. Nail every 6 inches around the perimeter of each sheet, and every 12 inches along inter-mediate supports. Be careful not to dimple the wood surface with the last hammer blow.

Installing plywood sheet siding

TOOLKIT
- Tape measure
- Chalk line
- Circular saw
- Carpenter's level
- Claw hammer
- Caulking gun
- Carpenter's square (optional)

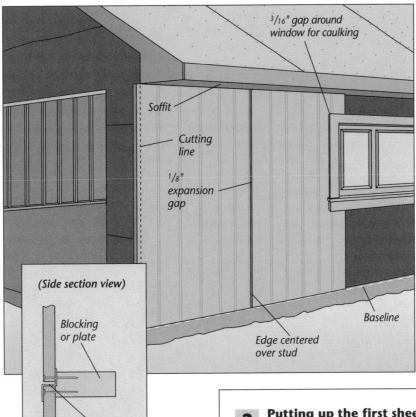

(Side section view)

Blocking or plate

Horizontal Z-flashing

Plywood siding

$^3/_{16}$" gap around window for caulking

Soffit

Cutting line

$^1/_8$" expansion gap

Baseline

Edge centered over stud

1 Cutting to length
Before you begin put-ting up panels, you'll need to determine their correct lengths; they should reach from the base chalk line to the soffit *(left)*. Should the distance from baseline to soffit be longer than the plywood sheets, you'll need to join panels end to end. Protect the horizontal seams with horizontal Z-flashing *(inset)*. In any case, brush all the panel edges with a sealant before installation.

2 Putting up the first sheet
To begin your installation, position the first sheet at an outside corner, its bottom edge flush with the base-line. Use a carpenter's level to check that the vertical edges are plumb. If the corner itself isn't plumb, you'll need to trim the plywood edge to align with it. The inside vertical edge must be centered over a stud, furring strip, or other firm backing. Hold or tack the sheet in place, flush with the baseline, and trace along the outer-most points of the existing siding or framing from top to bottom. Take the panel down and cut along this line. Nail the trimmed panel in place.

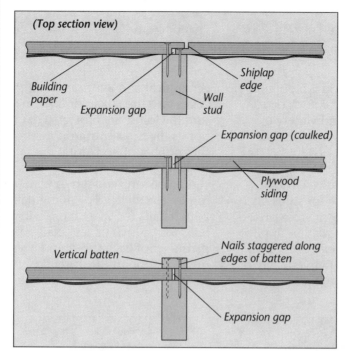

(Top section view)

Building paper

Expansion gap

Wall stud

Shiplap edge

Expansion gap (caulked)

Plywood siding

Vertical batten

Nails staggered along edges of batten

Expansion gap

3 Putting up successive sheets

The next sheet butts against the first sheet, often with an overlapping shiplap vertical edge *(left, top)*. Leave a 1/8" expansion gap at all joints. Sheets must join over studs, blocking, or other sturdy backing. Be careful not to nail through the laps.

If your plywood doesn't have a shiplap edge, caulk along vertical edges and butt them loosely, leaving about 1/8" for expansion *(left, middle)*. You can also cover the joints with 1x2 strips called battens *(left, bottom);* this is a must if there's no building paper behind the joint.

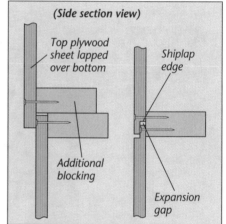

(Side section view)

Top plywood sheet lapped over bottom

Shiplap edge

Additional blocking

Expansion gap

ASK A PRO

WHAT IF I CHOOSE A HORIZONTAL PATTERN?
When installing plywood siding with a horizontal pattern, stagger vertical end joints and nail the long, horizontal edges into fire blocks or other nailing supports. Protect horizontal seams with metal Z-flashing (page 71), by overlapping, or by choosing panels with shiplap edges (right).

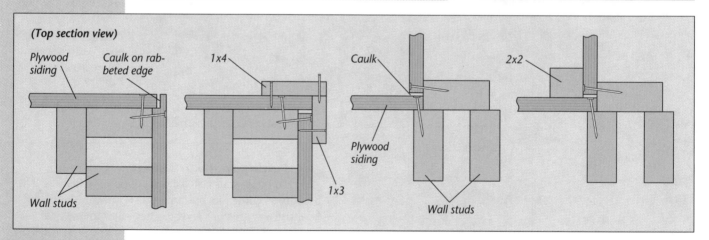

(Top section view)

Plywood siding

Caulk on rabbeted edge

Wall studs

1x4

1x3

Caulk

Plywood siding

Wall studs

2x2

4 Dealing with corners

Plywood siding requires special corner construction to ensure a weathertight joint. Outside corners can either be rabbeted together and caulked *(above, far left)*, or covered by a 1x3 and 1x4 trim board *(above left)*; leave a 1/8" gap for expansion.

Inside corners are generally just caulked and butted together *(above right)*, although you can also supply a vertical corner trim board, such as a 2x2 *(above, far right)*. If the plywood is milled with grooves, the grooves under corner boards might let dirt and water penetrate. To prevent this, nail the vertical trim boards directly to the corner studs or siding, caulk along the edges, and butt the plywood against them.

5 Cutting for windows and doors

When you're cutting out these large areas, remember the carpenter's maxim, "Measure twice, cut once." If possible, center the seams between sheets over or under the opening. Lay out the cuts with a carpenter's square or chalk line, then make the cuts. If you're using a saber saw for cutting corners and curves, cut the sheets on the back side to avoid splintering the face, since these saws cut on the upstroke. (When you're laying out the lines, beware: the sheet will be flipped over when installed.)

SOFFITS

A soffit (sometimes called cornice) is the underside of the rafters and roof at the eaves. As shown below, soffits can be left open or closed. To close a soffit, you can either use specially constructed vinyl or aluminum panels—available commercially—or wood. Vinyl and aluminum soffit coverings are installed with support channels mounted on the fascia and wall of the structure. The panels are slid into grooves in the channels and joined at interlocking edges.

If you close your soffits, you'll need to install vents to provide air circulation in the enclosed space. Vinyl and aluminum soffit coverings are designed to permit air flow through perforated panels spaced every 10 feet or so along the soffit's length; follow the manufacturer's instructions. For wood, you'll need to cut holes in the panels with a jig saw or hole saw to install square or circular vents. In this case, it's best to consult your local building code for spacing requirements.

Finishing the soffit

TOOLKIT

- Circular saw
- Combination square
- Claw hammer
- Chalk line
- Tape measure

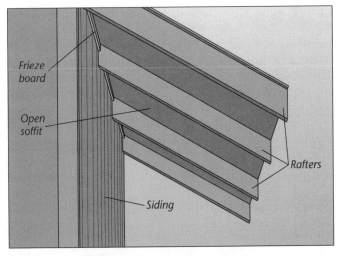

Frieze board

Open soffit

Siding

Rafters

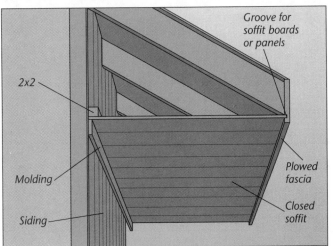

2x2

Molding

Siding

Groove for soffit boards or panels

Plowed fascia

Closed soffit

Finishing the soffit

When leaving a soffit open, cut the siding so it extends to the very top of the wall; notch it where it intersects the rafters. Install a frieze board—molding or a narrow trim board—along the top edge *(left, above)*.

If you prefer a closed soffit, you can buy or make a plowed fascia board—a board with a routed groove near one edge for holding soffit boards or panels—and nail it over the rafter ends *(left, below)*. To complete the closed soffit, mark a point at both ends of the wall, level with the top of the groove in the fascia board. Snap a chalk line between the two marks; then nail a 2x2 above the chalk line. Measure the distance from the interior of the groove to the wall. Cut the soffit boards to fit; then install them in the plowed fascia and nail them to the bottom of the 2x2. Hide the nails with molding, fastening it with galvanized finishing nails set below the surface.

Most exterior surfaces require a finish, both for appearance and protection from the elements. There are two main types of exterior finishes, latex (water-base) and alkyd (solvent- or oil-base). Latex products are easily applied, and can be cleaned and thinned with water. They are considered less harmful, both to people and to the environment, than alkyds. Some states have laws requiring lower levels of volatile organic compounds (VOCs) in finishes. Alkyd products contain high levels of VOCs; latex products also contain VOCs, but at much lower levels. In areas with strict VOC regulations, you'll only find products that comply; elsewhere, you may have a choice.

Paints: A good choice for less-attractive lumber, paints offer uniform coverage—even the grain will not be visible—in a choice of colors to match your house. Latex paints are available in as wide a range of colors and finishes (flat, semigloss, and gloss) as alkyd paints, and will perform slightly better; in fact some siding manufacturers recommend against using alkyd paints. Expect a good-quality latex paint to last about five years.

Stains: An alternative to paint, stains are an attractive choice, especially for decorative shakes and shingles. Stains are generally available in two color intensities. Semitransparent types contain enough pigment to tint the wood, but not enough to hide the natural grain. Solid-color stains (also called heavy-bodied stains) contain more pigment; many are almost as opaque as paint. Some manufacturers offer a third option: transparent stains with very subtle amounts of color. These stains are intended for use with attractive, naturally decay-resistant wood products, such as cedar shingles; they tend to enhance or intensify the color of the wood while providing extra protection from weathering.

Application: Experts recommend applying a finish to a garage or shed using a brush or roller, rather than a sprayer. The job may be time-consuming, but these tools are inexpensive, easy to use, and deliver the finish where you want it, rather than on the surrounding area. Paint sprayers of various type can be obtained from tool-rental shops, but they require practice for effective use.

Choose the correct type of brush for the finish you're applying: Synthetic bristle brushes are suitable for most types of paint or stain; natural bristle brushes should be used only with alkyd paints. The better the quality of the brush, the better the finish. A good brush is less likely to leave its bristles in the paint.

For rollers, the nap thickness you need depends on the texture of the surface you're covering: Choose a thick nap for heavily textured surfaces, such as shakes, or a thinner nap for smooth surfaces, such as plywood siding.

Both brushes and rollers come in various widths, allowing you to paint in corners and niches, or cover a large area with fewer strokes. Be sure the paint trays are wide enough to accommodate the rollers you choose.

Cover the surrounding area with drop cloths (use 6-mil polyethylene or old sheets). To avoid splatters with a roller, don't roll too vigorously. With a brush, gently lift it away from the surface at the end of each stroke. Smooth surfaces require less paint than textured, and some surfaces absorb more stain than others; read the product label for approximate coverage.

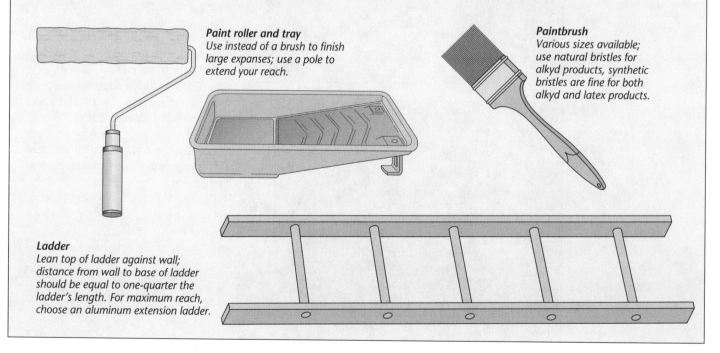

Paint roller and tray
Use instead of a brush to finish large expanses; use a pole to extend your reach.

Paintbrush
Various sizes available; use natural bristles for alkyd products, synthetic bristles are fine for both alkyd and latex products.

Ladder
Lean top of ladder against wall; distance from wall to base of ladder should be equal to one-quarter the ladder's length. For maximum reach, choose an aluminum extension ladder.

GUTTER SYSTEMS

Roofs shed water, but gutters and downspouts carry the water away. Most gutters and downspouts are made of galvanized steel, aluminum, or vinyl, though you may find some made from wood or copper. Metal and wood types can be painted. Professionally installed gutters are often extruded on site so they'll be seamless. But systems you can assemble and install yourself of preformed parts—U-shaped troughs, elbows, downspouts, and connectors—do as good a job if properly installed and maintained. The parts of a typical system are illustrated below.

Gutters are attached to the eaves of the house with strap, bracket, or spike-and-ferrule hangers. Strap hangers are nailed onto the roof underneath the roofing material. It's best to install them before the starter course of roofing material is laid, although with asphalt-shingle roofs, they can sometimes be installed after roofing. Bracket hangers and spike-and-ferrule hangers are mounted on the fascia boards. Downspouts are attached by straps to exterior walls.

To work effectively, gutters and downspouts must be in good condition, must slope at the correct angle, and must be kept free of debris.

Gutters come in 4-, 5-, and 6-inch diameters; downspouts are available in 3- and 4-inch diameters. The size you use depends on the square footage of each section of the roof, as shown in the chart below.

Most manufacturers sell gutters in 10-foot lengths. Estimate the number of lengths you'll need based on the length of the eaves. Also count the number of fasteners and other fittings you'll need—including one connector for each length, caps for each end, inside or outside corners for each turn, one drop outlet and three straps for each downspout, and one hanger for every three feet of gutter. If your roof has overhangs, you'll also need elbows to connect each downspout to its drop outlet. For vinyl gutters, you may also need polyvinyl chloride (PVC) cement to attach the pieces.

Metal gutters can be cut with a hacksaw; for vinyl gutters, use a fine-toothed handsaw. File down any rough edges.

GUTTER SIZE AND DOWNSPOUT DIAMETER

Roof area (square feet)	Gutter size	Downspout diameter
100-800	4"	3"
800-1000	5"	3"
1000-1400	5"	4"
1400+	6"	4"

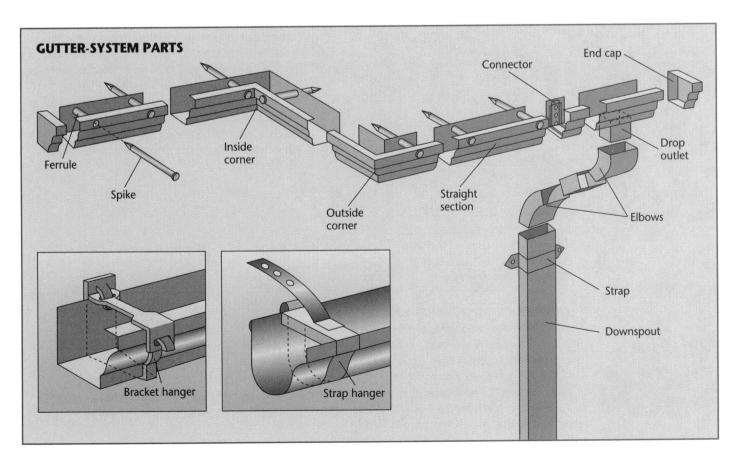

GUTTER-SYSTEM PARTS

Ferrule · Spike · Inside corner · Outside corner · Straight section · Connector · End cap · Drop outlet · Elbows · Strap · Downspout

Bracket hanger · Strap hanger

Installing a gutter system

TOOLKIT
- Chalk line
- Line level
- Caulking gun
- Claw hammer
- Electric drill with masonry bit (optional)

1 ▶ Determining the slope
To mark the proper slope for a gutter system, position a chalk line immediately below where the gutter will be located, and tie it to nails at each end. Use a line level to level the string *(right)*, then lower the string at the downspout end to achieve a drop of 1" per 20'. For lengths over 35', the gutter should slope both ways from the center *(inset)*. Snap the chalk line.

2 Assembling the gutter
Metal gutter parts either snap together or join with connectors. Caulk along both the inside of the connector and the undersides of the gutter sections, then push the ends together. Caulk joints and end caps.

Some vinyl systems use PVC cement, but don't glue the downspouts to the drop outlets, or you won't be able to remove them when they require cleaning.

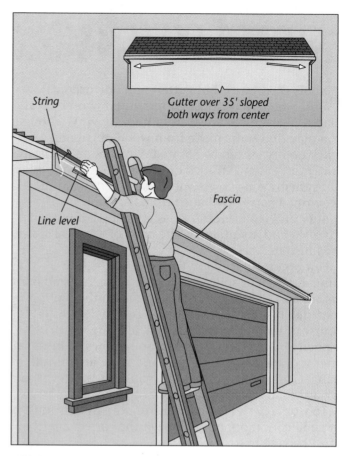

Gutter over 35' sloped both ways from center

String

Line level

Fascia

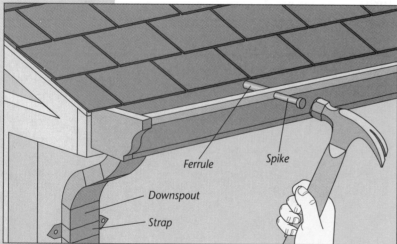

Ferrule

Spike

Downspout

Strap

3 Fastening gutters to the roof
Align the gutter with the chalk line on the garage. Nail the first hangers at the downspout end, taking care to position the downspout correctly. Working outward from that point, fasten the gutter in place with one hanger every 3'; use two hangers at each corner for support.

Secure the downspouts to the wall with straps; use nails or screws for wood siding, expanding anchor bolts in masonry. Coat the back of each strap with caulking compound or roofing cement to produce a seal.

 ASK A PRO

HOW CAN I IMPROVE DRAINAGE?
To divert water coming from your downspouts away from your building, place a ready-made concrete or plastic splash block below an elbow attached to the downspout. Tilt the block so the water flows away from the house.

Or, you can choose a plastic or fabric sleeve that you attach directly to the downspout. Some sleeves are perforated to disperse the water over a large area; others unroll as the water flows through them, diverting drainage away from the house; the sleeve rolls back up once the water has drained.

GARAGE DOORS

Although installing a garage door may be the trick-iest of all tasks when building your own garage, there's no reason why it's a job you can't handle your-self—providing you follow the installation instructions closely. This section will show you how to install a typical roll-up door *(below)*. As with the automatic garage door opener featured on page 81, the installation instructions are specific to a certain model. Always consult your owner's manual.

A roll-up, or sectional, door is the most common type of garage door on the market. It moves up and down on rollers housed in channeled tracks. A torsion spring across the top of the door, or extension springs along the sides, helps when lifting or lowering the door. Although the latter system is easier and safer to install, a torsion spring *(page 80)* requires less regular adjustment once it's in place.

Regardless of the type of spring you choose, it's best to maintain your door, cleaning the tracks, hinges, and rollers and lubricating them with penetrating oil or silicone spray on a regular basis. As well, tighten the screws on the hardware, and use powdered graphite on the lock. Keep the door sealed and painted to prevent moisture damage.

Apart from roll-up doors, swing-up or one-piece doors are also available. These pivot on hinges and usually have springs on each side to adjust the balance. (NOTE: The hinges on swing-up doors tend to come unbalanced, causing the door to scrape against the sides of the frame. It's best to periodically check for this, adjusting when necessary.) Swing-up doors, however, don't provide as much clearance as the roll-up type. In a garage with 8 feet of headroom, a few extra inches are typically lost when the door is fully open. And because swing-up doors swing to the out-side, they can become easily damaged by objects situated too close to the door. Always keep the area in front of the door free from obstruction.

Chain-drive automatic door openers, the most common, should have a return switch so the door will reverse automatically when it meets obstacles. If the door doesn't open or close completely, won't stay open, or won't reverse, you can make adjustments to the opener following the manufacturer's instructions. Be sure to always test the door carefully after the adjustment. Follow the instructions on installing garage doors and openers over the next pages, and consult a professional if you run into any problems.

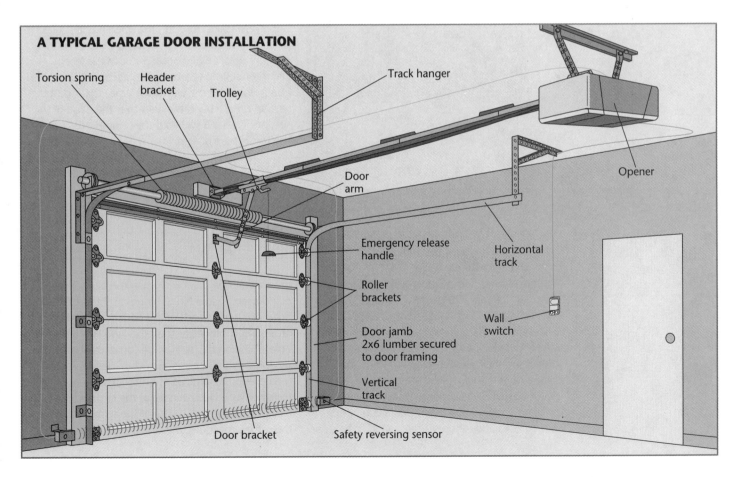

A TYPICAL GARAGE DOOR INSTALLATION

Torsion spring · Header bracket · Trolley · Track hanger · Door arm · Opener · Emergency release handle · Horizontal track · Roller brackets · Wall switch · Door jamb 2x6 lumber secured to door framing · Vertical track · Door bracket · Safety reversing sensor

Assembling the door

TOOLKIT
- Ratchet set or wrench for sheet metal screws
- Carpenter's level
- Claw hammer
- Drill (optional)

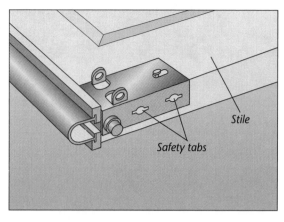

Stile

Safety tabs

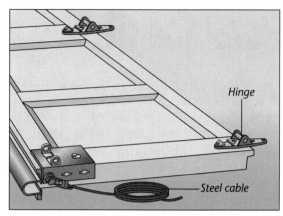

Hinge

Steel cable

1 Preparing the first door section

Begin by laying the hardware out on the floor of the garage so you can easily see all the pieces. Find the bottom door section, which has an aluminum weatherstrip retainer along its bottom edge, then place this section face down on the floor. Fit the bottom brackets on each bottom corner of the section, making sure the slots on the end stile line up with the safety tabs in the bracket *(above, left)*. Secure the brackets to the door stiles with #14x⅜"

sheet metal screws. Then, hook the ends of the steel cable over the protrusions on the brackets. Fasten No. 1 hinges—numbers are stamped on the sides of the hinges corresponding to their location on the door—to the predrilled holes along the top edge of the door section *(above, right)*. If you need a reinforcing strut, attach it on top of the hinges, using screws and the clips provided.

Jamb

3" nail

Jamb

2 Positioning the bottom section

Position the bottom section in the door opening so that it is centered, level, and rests against the stop molding tacked flush to the inside of the jamb. (The stop molding will prevent the door from falling through the opening. It's nailed in position once the door is installed.) Use a wood shim to adust any inconsistencies in the level. Hammer a 3" nail partway into each side jamb, about one-third the way down from the top of the section *(inset)*; bend the nails over the edge of the section. The nails will hold the door in position until the tracks are installed.

3 Preparing and installing the middle sections

Find the second door section and set it face down on the floor. For doors with locks, the second section can be identified by the predrilled lock assembly holes in the center of the panel. If you have no lock assembly, lock templates for positioning the holes are available from your garage door manufacturer. In either case, install the lock assembly according to the manufacturer's instructions. NOTE: For doors equipped with automatic door openers *(page 81)*, the door

must always be unlocked when the opener is being used. Fasten No. 2 hinges at the predrilled holes on the top ends of the door section, then fasten No. 1 hinges to the other two sets of holes. Position this section on top of the bottom section. Hold it in position with 3" nails hammered into the jambs. Fasten the two sections together with No. 2 hinges at the ends, and No. 1 hinges at the middle of the section. Follow the same procedure to install the third section.

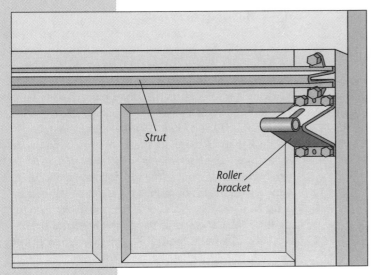

Strut

Roller bracket

4 Attaching the top section

Lay the top section on the floor, then fit the roller brackets over the predrilled holes at the top corner of the panel. Attach each bracket with sheet metal screws *(left)*. If your door requires a strut for added support, attach it to the top section with strut clips. NOTE: With wider doors, it may also be necessary to attach struts on other sections; check the manufacturer's instructions. Mount the top section on the rest of the door, holding it in place with nails in the jambs, and join it to the section below it by attaching the hinges. Install rollers in the top and bottom brackets, as well as in the tube openings in each of the hinges.

Assembling the track

TOOLKIT
- Ratchet set
- Screwdriver
- Hacksaw
- Tape measure
- Drill
- Claw hammer

1 Installing the vertical track

Connect each track bracket to the vertical track with one ¼"x⅝" track bolt and ¼" flange nut *(below)*. Make sure the flat side of the track faces the wall. Using the same size nuts and bolts, attach the flag bracket to the top of the track *(inset)*. Then, using both hands to hold the track, place it over the rollers on the door, moving it toward the center of the door to push the rollers all the way into the hinges; there should be a ⅜" space between the edge of the door and the track. Lift the track about ½" and screw the flag bracket and track brackets to the jamb with ⁵⁄₁₆"x1⅝" lag screws. Tighten the track bolts and flange nuts. If the tops of the track aren't level with one another, cut a small piece from the bottom of one track and lower it; or, you can raise the other track. Don't raise it past the rollers on the bottom of the door.

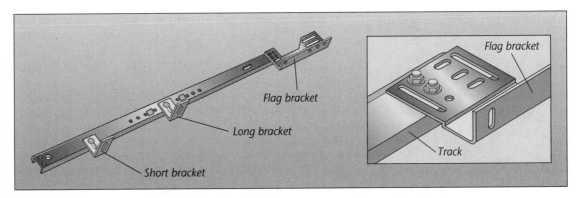

Flag bracket

Long bracket

Short bracket

Flag bracket

Track

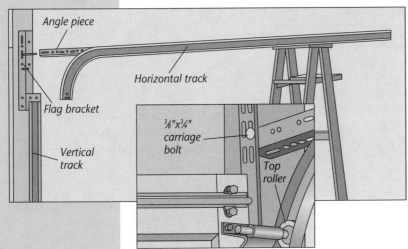

Angle piece

Horizontal track

Flag bracket

Vertical track

⅜"x¾" carriage bolt

Top roller

2 Installing the horizontal track

Assemble the horizontal track by first attaching the angle piece to the main track with ¼"x⅝" track bolts and ¼" flange nuts. Support the rear end of the track on a ladder *(left)*. Place the horizontal track over the top bracket's roller, then attach the track's curved end to the flag bracket using the same size track bolts and flange nuts mentioned above. Bolt the end of the angle piece to the top of the flag bracket with a ⅜"x¾" carriage bolt and ⅜" hex nut *(inset)*. The two tracks, horizontal and vertical, must form a single, smooth channel for the rollers. Follow the same procedure for the other side.

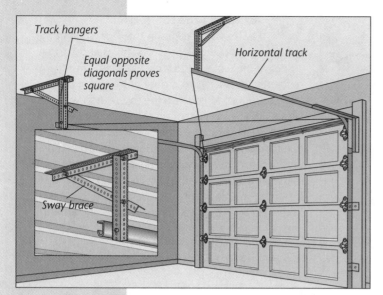

Track hangers

Equal opposite diagonals proves square

Horizontal track

Sway brace

3 Hanging the track

Buy enough 13 gauge or ³⁄₃₂" prepunched metal angle to make two rear track hangers. Using the illustration at left *(inset)* as a guide, cut the metal into three pieces. Use ³⁄₈"x1" bolts (and nuts) to join two lengths so they form a right angle; add a third piece, a sway brace, to connect the two as shown. Use the same size nuts and bolts to attach the hangers to the ends of the tracks.

Check that the tracks are square by measuring the distances from the top left corner of the door to the end of the right horizontal track, and the top right corner of the door to the end of the left horizontal track. If the two measurements aren't within ½" of each other, the tracks need to be adjusted. The tracks should be roughly level, but the distance from the tracks to the joists can differ up to 1" from the front jamb to the rear hangers. Finally, drill pilot holes and fasten the hangers to the joists with ⁵⁄₁₆"x1½" lag screws.

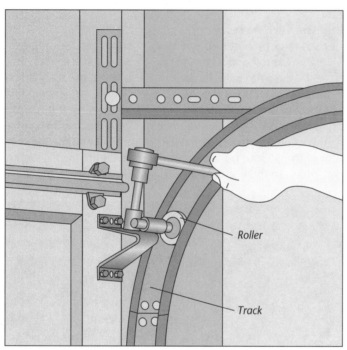

Roller

Track

4 Making final adjustments

Adjust the top door section by loosening the slide on the top bracket, then forcing the top of the door against the stop molding on the door jamb. Pull the roller toward you so that it's secure against the groove in the track and tighten the slide bolts *(left)*.

Once the adjustments are complete, finish the door's lock assembly. Attach the lock spring latches and striker plates, lock bar, lock cables, or slide bolt (whichever is preferred), according to the manufacturer's instructions. (If you plan to install an automatic garage door opener, follow the instructions beginning on the opposite page.) Remove the 3" nails from the door jambs. To install the torsion springs, see below.

 PLAY IT SAFE

HAVE A PROFESSIONAL INSTALL THE TORSION SPRING MECHANISM

Torsion springs are vital to the operation of a garage door. They help to open and close the door and keep it balanced in a semi-open position. Typically, a 16'x7' steel door requires two torsion springs connected together, as shown below, each supporting 60 to 80 foot pounds of pressure when the door is fully closed. Although vital, torsion springs can be difficult and dangerous to install or repair, requiring special winding tools. Always call a professional.

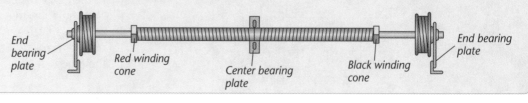

End bearing plate

Red winding cone

Center bearing plate

Black winding cone

End bearing plate

Assembling a garage door opener

TOOLKIT

- Ratchet set
- Screwdriver

1 Assembling the T-rail and trolley

Place the three T-rail sections on a level work surface, with the arrow label on the center section pointing toward the door. Use the rail braces to join the sections together *(below, left)*, attaching them with the carriage bolts and nuts provided. To avoid obstructing the trolley, make sure that the nuts are on the brace side of the rail. Position the cable pulley bracket on the front end of the T-rail. Ensuring that the bracket is parallel to the rail, fasten it in place with hex screws, lock washers, and nuts *(below, inset)*. Next, attach the threaded shaft piece to the trolley with a lock washer and nut and position the trolley on the track. Install a temporary stop, such as a screwdriver, in the hole in the front end of the T-rail, *(below, right)*. Slide the trolley along the rail to make sure it runs smoothly.

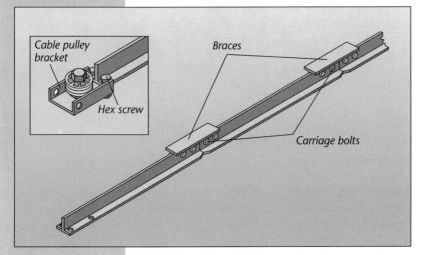

Cable pulley bracket
Hex screw
Braces
Carriage bolts

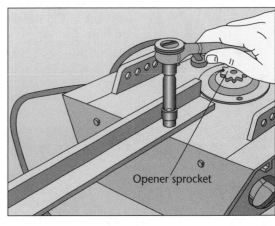

Screwdriver
Threaded shaft
Cable pulley bracket
Trolley

2 Attaching the T-rail to the opener

So as not to damage the cover of the opener, lay a pad down on the work surface and place the opener on it. Place a support under the cable pulley bracket. Remove the two screws from the top of the opener and put them aside. Align the holes in the T-rail with the holes in the opener, then securely fasten the rail with the screws *(right)*. Insert a hex screw, which will limit trolley travel in the up direction, into the T-rail's trolley stop hole; attach a lock washer and nut and tighten.

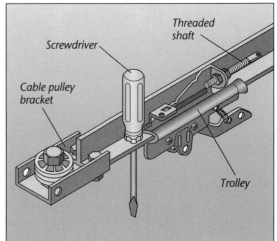

Opener sprocket

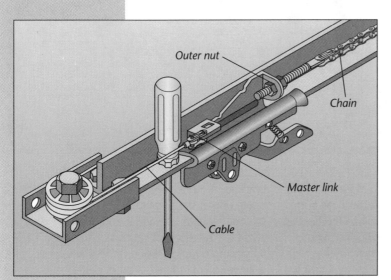

Outer nut
Chain
Master link
Cable

3 Connecting the chain and cable

Attach the cable loop to the trolley with a master link. The posts on the master link bar fit up through the cable loop and hole in the front of the trolley. A cap covers the posts and a clip-on spring holds the assembly together. Run the cable around the pulley and back toward the sprocket on the opener. The chain should begin feeding out of the package. Hooking the chain to the teeth around the sprocket, run it toward the threaded shaft on the trolley. Use the second master link to connect the chain to the shaft *(left)*; remove the screwdriver. Attach the sprocket cover to the mounting plate on the opener. Tighten the chain and cable assembly by turning the outer nut on the threaded shaft clockwise; you'll need to back off the inner nut to do this. The chain should be ½" above the rail at its midpoint.

Installing the opener

TOOLKIT

- Tape measure
- Electric drill with ⅜₆" bit
- Ratchet set
- Hacksaw

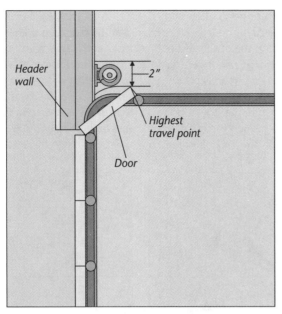

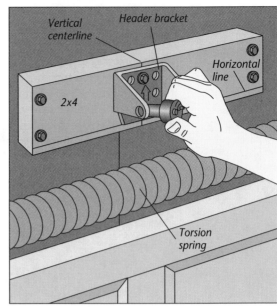

1 Installing the header bracket

With the garage door closed, find its vertical centerline and mark it on the header wall. (If a torsion spring will be in the way, you can draw the vertical line 2' left or right of center.) Next, open the door and draw a horizontal line on the header wall 2" higher than the highest door travel point *(above, left).* This will allow clearance for the door's top edge. Clearance brackets are available if headroom is less than 2". Center a 2x4 on the wall where the vertical and horizontal lines intersect, and fasten it to the studs with lag screws; draw the two lines across the face of the 2x4. Center the header bracket on the 2x4 at the vertical line with its bottom edge on the horizontal line. Mark the holes for the bracket and drill ⅜₆" pilot holes. Attach the bracket to the 2x4 with lag screws *(above, right).*

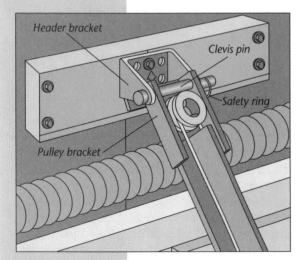

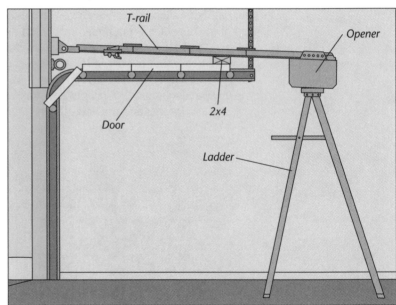

2 Positioning the unit

Place the opener on packing material on the floor below the header bracket. Lift the T-rail and align the pulley bracket with the hole in the header bracket. (If the torsion spring is in the way, you may have to move the opener away from the door and place it on a chair to achieve a better angle so the T-rail clears the spring.) To connect the two brackets, insert a clevis pin in the hole and attach a safety ring at the end of the pin *(above, left).* Place the opener on a stepladder and open the door. Lay a 2x4 on the top door section beneath the T-rail. By placing scraps of wood under the opener, raise or lower it until there is a bit of clearance between the T-rail and the 2x4 *(above, right).*

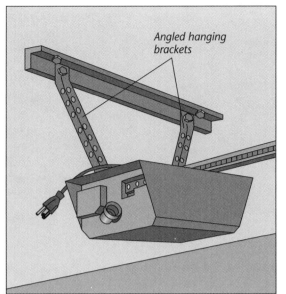

Angled hanging brackets

3 Hanging the opener

Drill holes in a length of angle iron and fasten it across the ceiling joists. Measure the distance from the top of the opener to the angle iron and cut two hanging brackets—perforated metal strapping is fine—to length. The brackets should be set angled from the top of the unit to the ceiling, as shown. (If the joists are exposed, you can fasten the hanging brackets directly to the joists using lag screws; drill pilot holes first.) Bolt one end of each bracket to the angle iron, then attach the opener to the hanging brackets using the screws, lock washers, and nuts provided. Make sure the T-rail is in line with the header bracket. Remove the 2x4 from on top of the door support. If the door hits the rail when you open it manually, raise the header bracket. Grease the top and underside of the rail surface where the trolley will slide.

Installing the control console

TOOLKIT
• Tape measure
• Wire stripper
• Screwdriver
• Electric drill

Making the connection

The door control, typically attached to the wall, should be at least 5' above the floor, and away from all moving parts. Console models may be mounted to a standard single conductor box. Strip ¼" of insulation from one end of the bell wire, then connect the white wire to the No. 2 terminal screw on the back of the door control, and the white/red wire to the No. 1 terminal screw (right). Remove the control's cover with a screwdriver and fasten the console to the wall by screwing through the pre-drilled holes; replace the cover. Connect the bell wire

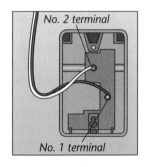

No. 2 terminal

No. 1 terminal

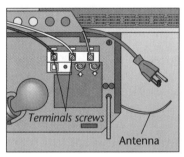

Terminals screws

Antenna

to the terminal screws on the right side of the opener panel (above, right). For remote control, position the antenna wire as shown. Screw light bulbs into the sockets on the sides of the opener.

Installing the sensor

TOOLKIT
• Screwdriver
• Ratchet set
• Tape measure
• Electric drill
• Wire stripper

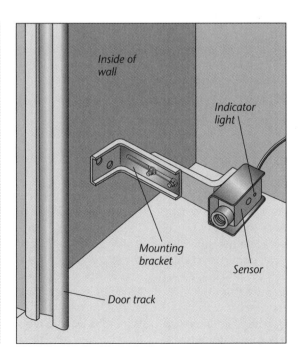

Inside of wall

Indicator light

Mounting bracket

Sensor

Door track

Connecting the assemblies

Assemble the mounting brackets for the sensors as shown in the illustration at left. Position one bracket over a stud on one side of the door 4"-6" above the floor. Mark the screw holes on the wall and remove the bracket to drill pilot holes at the marks. Use lag screws to attach the bracket to the stud. Mount the bracket on the other side of the door using the same procedure; make sure it's exactly the same height. Use the hex bolts and wing nuts supplied to secure each sensor unit to the bracket so their lenses point at each other across the door; leave the wing nut loose on one sensor for final adjustment. Run the wires from both sensors to the opener, stripping ¼" insulation from each set of wires. Connect the white wires to the No. 2 terminal screw, and the white/black wires to the No. 3 screw. With the lock feature off, plug in the opener. Once the green indicator lights in both sensors glow, they are in alignment; tighten the wing nut on the other sensor.

Connecting the door to the opener

TOOLKIT
- Tape measure
- Knife to cut rope
- Electric drill
- Ratchet set

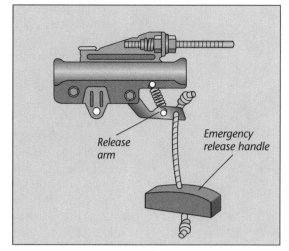

Release arm

Emergency release handle

1 Attaching the emergency release

Cut a piece of rope to 6" in length. Thread one end of the rope through the emergency release handle and tie a knot at least 1" from the end. Thread the other end of the rope through the hole in the release arm of the trolley. Once attached to the trolley, the handle should hang 6' above the floor. You may need to adjust the rope. NOTE: Never use the emergency handle to pull the door open or closed, as the knot could untie; the handle should only be used to disengage the trolley when the door is closed.

2 Attaching the bracket to the door

For aluminum, steel, glass, or fiberglass panel garage doors, added horizontal and vertical reinforcement may be needed; refer to your owner's manual. You can use angle irons or get a door reinforcement kit from your garage door manufacturer. If your door does not need reinforcing, use carriage bolts, lock washers, and nuts to install the door bracket and door bracket plate 2"-4" below the top edge of the door centered below the header bracket (right). NOTE: When drilling holes through the door for the carriage bolts, be careful not to damage the face of the door.

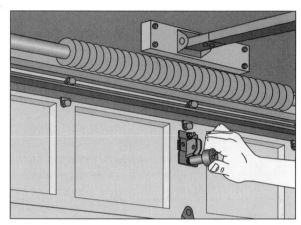

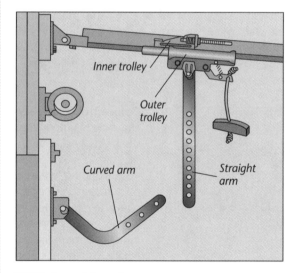

Inner trolley

Outer trolley

Curved arm

Straight arm

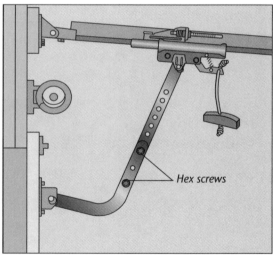

Hex screws

3 Attaching the arms

With the door fully closed, pull the emergency release handle to disconnect the outer trolley from the inner trolley. Slide the outer trolley about 2" away from the door. Using a clevis pin and safety ring, attach the straight door arm to the outer trolley section. Fasten the curved door arm to the door bracket with hex screws, washers, and nuts (above, left). Then line up the holes and bring the two arms together.

If the straight arm is too long and extends past the edge of the curved arm, remove it from the trolley and cut it back from the end. Reconnect the straight arm to the trolley, bring the arm sections together, and line up the holes again. Fasten the arms securely to each other with hex screws, lock washers, and nuts (above, right). When the opener is activated, the outer and inner trollies will come together automatically.

Making adjustments

TOOLKIT
• Screwdriver

Adjusting the up/down limits

The limit adjustment settings are found on the left side panel of the opener. If anything interferes with the door as it is opening, it will stop; an obstacle will cause the door to reverse direction when closing. First check if the door opens and closes properly. With the door closed, press the open button on the wall control panel. If it opens at least 5', but not completely, use a screwdriver to turn the up limit adjustment screw clockwise; one turn equals 2" of travel. If the door doesn't open at least 5', read the instructions at right. Next, press the down button on the control panel. If the door won't close, increase the down travel limit by turning the down adjustment screw counterclockwise. Decrease the down limit if the door reverses when fully closed. If there's no interference yet the door reverses when closing, check for any obstruction of the reversing sensor. If the sensors are free from obstruction—lights are not flashing on the opener—increase the down force.

Adjusting the force

Force adjustment settings regulate the power needed to open and close the door. Controls are on the right side panel of the opener. Don't increase the force beyond the minimum needed to close the door; too much force will interfere with its proper operation. On the other hand, forces set too low can cause nuisance reversals in the down direction and stops in the up direction. Press the down button on the control panel to close the door. While it's on its way down, grab the bottom (be sure to stay out of the path of the sensors). If it doesn't reverse, decrease the down force. Increase the down force if the door reverses automatically while closing. To adjust the up force, grab hold of the bottom of the door as it's opening (again, staying out of the path of the sensors). If the door doesn't stop, decrease the up force. If it doesn't open at least 5', increase the up force slightly. If you have any trouble adjusting the force or limits on your door, call a service professional.

Testing the safety reversing sensor

TOOLKIT
• Screwdriver

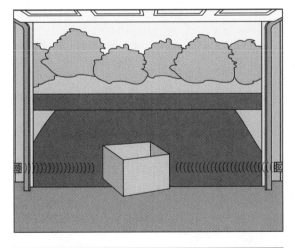

1 Checking the sensor
With the door completely open, place an obstacle, such as cardboard box, between the two sensors. Press the down button on the control panel to close the door. If the sensors have been installed properly, the door will not move more than 1" and the opener lights will flash. If the door does not stop right away, check to see that the sensors are aligned properly. If there is still a problem, call a service professional.

2 Testing the safety reverse system
Lay a 2x4 flat on the floor directly in the path of the open door. Press the down button on the control panel to close the door (left). If the door stops on the obstruction, but does not reverse, increase the down limit by turning the adjustment screw ¼ turn clockwise; repeat the test. The setting is fine when the door reverses on the 2x4. Once the reverse is set on the door, test the force and limits levels once again. Call a service professional if you can't get the door to reverse properly.

FINISHING THE INTERIOR

Once the exterior of your new shed or garage has been finished, it's time to give some thought to the inside. Obviously, you won't want to add the kind of features you would see in a house, or finish those that you do tackle with the same sort of exacting detail, but there are a few simple elements you can include that will make your new space both functional and comfortable.

This chapter starts by showing you the basic hookups for a wash sink and hose bibb, the two most common plumbing fixtures you'll find in a garage *(opposite)*. For tips on how to wire your space for electricity, use the wiring anatomy on page 88 as a guide; information on receptacles and switches, the keys to any electrical system, follows.

Once the plumbing and electricity have been installed, you may want to cover your wall and ceiling framing. One of the easiest ways to do this is to install gypsum wallboard. To cut the wallboard, secure it to the joists or studs, and finish the joints, turn to the steps starting on page 93. And although staircases are not common in most garages, you can easily build the set shown on page 99 if you need to provide access to an attic storage space or a second level.

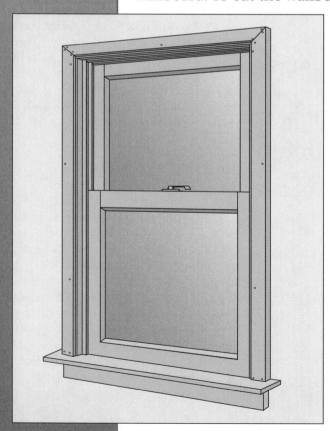

The edges of window openings need casing to cover gaps between the building materials and to add a finished look. To install the casing, or to trim other areas of an interior space, turn to page 96.

BASIC PLUMBING

Although it's unlikely that your garage or shed will have all the conveniences of a home, running water is probably one that you won't want to do without. A sink in the garage, for example, is ideal for cleaning gardening tools or washing up after working on the car. An outdoor faucet (hose bibb) provides an easy garden hose hookup for watering the lawn or flower beds.

As mentioned in the planning section of this book *(page 16)*, almost any job that adds pipe to an existing plumbing system will require approval from local building department officials before you start, and inspection of the work when you're finished. Learn what work you may do yourself—a few codes require that certain work be done only by licensed plumbers. When working with pipe, there are generally two types you can choose from: copper, shown at right, or plastic. Average do-it-yourselfers might find plastic piping easier to work with, although copper is much more durable.

When bringing water into a garage, remember that it will be a cold water supply branched from the main line supplying your house. The supply piping is laid before installing the slab *(page 23)*. If you choose to have hot water as well, such as for the sink hookup illustrated at right, you'll have to install a water heater in the garage and run the appropriate piping. The drain pipe for a sink, like the supply pipe, is installed before the slab is placed. Plan to have the supply pipe enter the garage through the slab and sole plate, or in front of the sole plate, as shown in the illustrations. Keep in mind that although the latter method may be less complicated, you should never situate a supply pipe in a place where it might get damaged, such as close to a parking space.

It's also smart to bring the supply pipe in as close to the fixtures as possible, this will save money—you won't have to run as much pipe—and hookup time. In this case the supply pipe brings the water directly to the hose bibb *(right, top)*, the highest-volume fixture in the installation. To branch off to the sink, you'll have to install a T-fitting.

Shutoff valves under the sink control the water supply through flexible riser tubes. The sink's drain connects to the main drain under the slab *(page 23)* with a roof stack venting the drainage system. You must install flashing around the stack, sealing it against the elements, before laying the final roofing material.

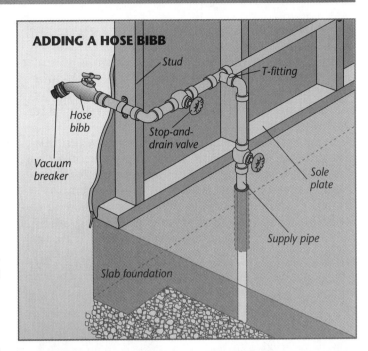

ADDING A HOSE BIBB

Stud
T-fitting
Hose bibb
Stop-and-drain valve
Vacuum breaker
Sole plate
Supply pipe
Slab foundation

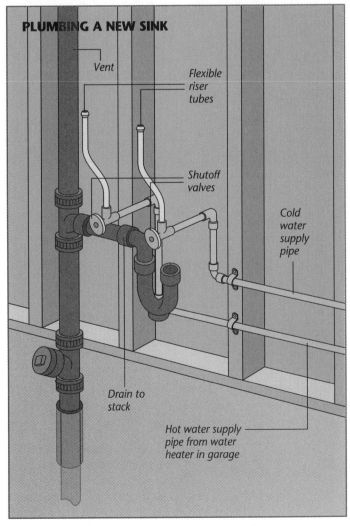

PLUMBING A NEW SINK

Vent
Flexible riser tubes
Shutoff valves
Cold water supply pipe
Drain to stack
Hot water supply pipe from water heater in garage

WIRING

When it comes to wiring a shed or a garage, the do-it-yourselfer can find comfort in the fact that electrical work is one of the easiest jobs to undertake. It's simple, neat, and logical, it doesn't require a shop full of specialized tools, and there's considerable standardization in home electrical systems and related materials.

The main wire that supplies the power will probably come from your home's service panel, connecting to a subpanel in your shed or garage *(page 24)*. (NOTE: This job must be done by an electrician.) Then, using the illustration below as a guide, you can set about wiring the structure; again, leaving the final hookup to the electrician. Never work on wiring that is "hot." Always check to make sure circuit breakers or fuses are off.

The following pages will show you how to wire switches, receptacles, and fixtures. Use wire strippers to expose wire from beneath the plastic insulation, and, when making connections, twist the wires together in a clockwise direction and add wire nuts.

All systems have hot wires—ungrounded conductors carrying the electrical current—and neutral wires—grounded conductors that complete a circuit by providing a return path to the source. Hot wires may have insulation of any color but are usually black or red, while neutral wires are always white or gray.

Routing new wiring

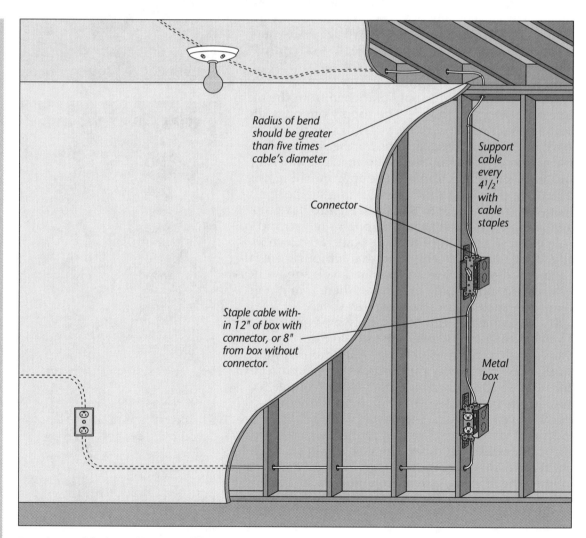

Radius of bend should be greater than five times cable's diameter

Support cable every 4$\frac{1}{2}$' with cable staples

Connector

Staple cable within 12" of box with connector, or 8" from box without connector.

Metal box

Routing cable in walls and ceilings
This illustration shows a typical route for running nonmetallic cable through a wall and ceiling. Run the cable through the studs and joists and fasten it in place with specially made cable staples. Drill holes for cable 1$\frac{1}{4}$" from the edge of wall studs; drill holes through the center of joists. NOTE: Where studs or rafters will be left exposed, you'll need to run the wire though a conduit; consult an electrician for this.

SWITCHES AND RECEPTACLES

Once a shed or a garage is wired, it's time to install switches and receptacles—the foot soldiers of any electrical system. Whether they're used to turn lights on and off, open automatic garage doors, or power up electric lawn mowers, switches and receptacles provide electricity where and when it's needed.

Switches control the flow of electrical current in a circuit. When a switch is turned ON, the circuit is closed and the electricity flows to a light or receptacle. When the switch is turned OFF, there is a break in the circuit with the electrical flow stopping at the switch.

All switches are rated according to the specific amperage and voltage for which they are suited. Switches marked CO-ALR can be used with either copper or aluminum wire. Unmarked switches and those marked CU-Al can be used with copper wire only. Always read the information stamped on a switch carefully and make sure the switch you are going to install is suitable for the circuit. Consult an electrician if you are in doubt.

The switch that is most commonly used in a shed or a garage is a single-pole switch. These switches have two terminals of the same color and a definite right side up. It makes no difference which hot (black) wire goes to which terminal.

Wires that are black, red, or any color other than white, green, or gray are always hot. But in some cases, a white wire may substitute as a hot (black) wire. In the example below *(right)*, the fixture is wired with a two-wire cable that is purchased with one black wire and one white wire. The white wire substitutes as the current-carrying wire going from the source to the switch. In this case, the end of the white wire is painted black to identify it as a hot wire.

Grounded receptacles consist of an upper and lower outlet with three slots. The larger (neutral) slot accepts the wire prong of a three-prong plug; the smaller (hot) slot is for the narrow prong, and the U-shaped grounding slot is for the grounding prong. The Code requires that all receptacles for 15- or 20-amp, 120-volt branch circuits be of the grounding type shown on pages 90 and 91. Some garages also have 240-volt circuits for power tools.

Common receptacles have three different colors of screw terminals. The brass-colored screws, on the side of the receptacle, are hot terminals; the white- or silver-colored screws, on the opposite side, are neutral terminals; and the green screw is the grounding terminal.

Like switches, all receptacles are rated for a specific amperage and voltage. This information is stamped clearly on the front of the receptacle.

This section will show you a few different ways of installing switches and receptacles. A single-pole switch installed at the end of a circuit is shown below. A switch in the middle of a circuit—or looped after a fixture in the middle of a circuit—is shown on page 90. A receptacle wired at the end of the circuit is also on page 90. To wire one receptacle to another, or a switch to a receptacle, turn to page 91. For some of these wiring configurations, you'll need three-wire cable.

Wiring single-pole switches

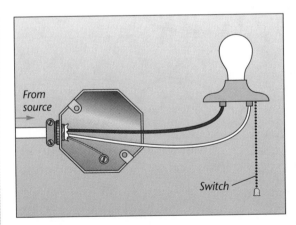

From source

Switch

Light at the end of a circuit
Use the following diagrams to guide you when installing a replacement switch and in planning a circuit extension. In the example above, the circuit ends at a light fixture controlled by a single-pole pull-chain switch. In the example at right, a single-pole wall switch is used to control a light at the end of the circuit.

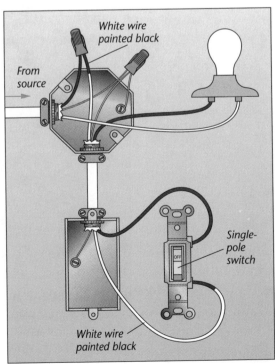

White wire painted black

From source

Single-pole switch

White wire painted black

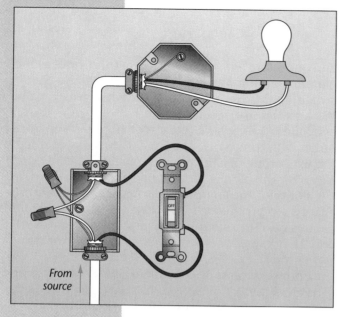

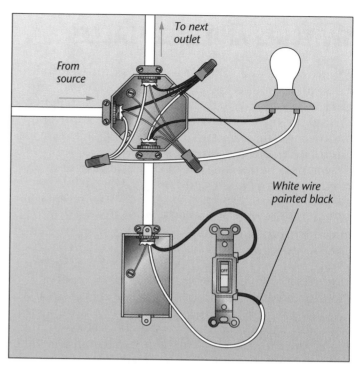

Switch in the middle of the circuit

In this wiring example, power goes through a single-pole switch that is located in the middle of a circuit (two or more cables enter the box). The switch controls a light at the end of the circuit.

Light in the middle of the circuit

In this example, the light is in the middle of a circuit (two or more cables enter the box) and the switch is wired in a switch loop. The switch controls the light in the middle of the circuit run.

Wiring a receptacle

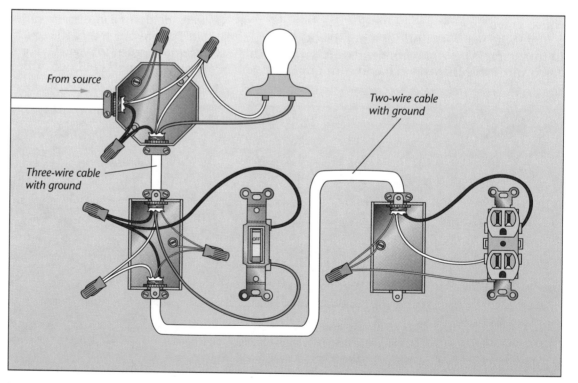

Receptacle after a switch

In this diagram, a switch is wired ahead of the receptacle in the circuit (two cables enter the switch box). The switch controls a light. The receptacle is at the end of the circuit (one cable enters the box). Both the upper and lower outlets of the receptacle are always hot.

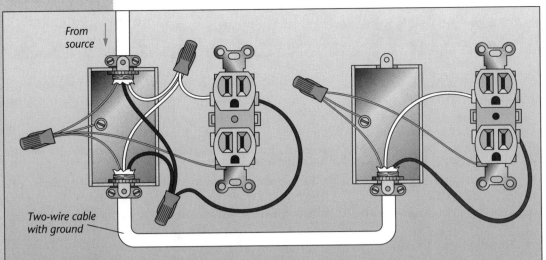

From source

Two-wire cable with ground

A second receptacle
In this example, the receptacles are wired parallel to each other in the same circuit. Both the upper and lower outlets of each receptacle are always hot.

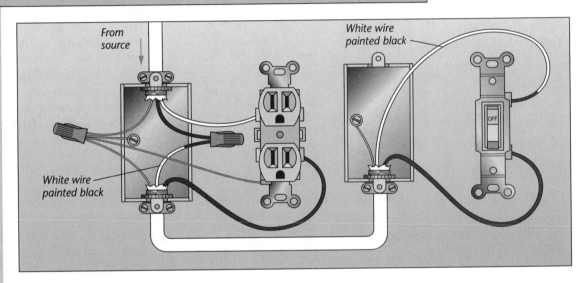

From source

White wire painted black

White wire painted black

Switch-controlled receptacle
Both the upper and lower outlets of this receptacle, located at the end of a circuit, are controlled by a single-pole switch. When the switch is on, the receptacle is hot; when the switch is off, the receptacle does not receive power.

 ASK A PRO

HOW DO I REPLACE A FLUORESCENT TUBE?
Fluorescent fixtures are a popular light source for garages. The tubes are brighter than bulbs, last about five times longer, emit less heat, and are easy to change.

To replace a double pin type tube, twist the old one a quarter turn in either direction and gently pull it out (right). Push the new tube into the tubeholders and give it a quarter turn. For a single pin type tube, push one end against the spring-loaded tubeholder and remove the other end; reverse the process to install a new tube.

ADDING INSULATION

If you want your garage to preserve warmth in winter or resist heat in the summer, insulation is the key. Of course, the best time to insulate is during the construction process, when the spaces between the joists, studs, and rafters are exposed. Mineral-fiber blankets or precut batts are the simplest types of insulation to apply in exposed areas. In general, insulating an unfinished attic *(below, bottom)* yields the greatest energy savings relative to its cost. Insulating the walls *(below, top)* is also very important.

You'll need a sharp utility knife for cutting the insulation blankets and a lightweight hand stapler for fastening them to the studs or joists. A step ladder is also handy for reaching high points on a wall or accessing an attic. To insulate in dark areas, you'll need at least one portable light.

Remember, insulation materials are either dusty or irritating to the skin, eyes, nose, and lungs. Wear gloves, a dust mask or respirator, eye protection, and long sleeves; tape the sleeves around your wrists.

Insulating the walls

TOOLKIT
• Tape measure
• Utility knife
• Hand stapler

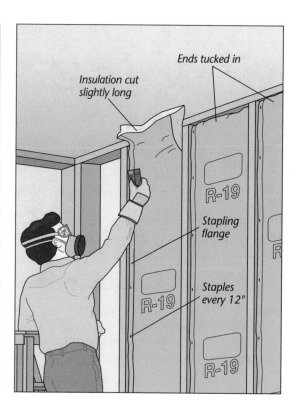

Insulation cut slightly long

Ends tucked in

R-19

Stapling flange

Staples every 12"

R-19

R-19

Installing insulation and vapor barriers
Precut 4' batts are simplest to handle when insulating a standard 8' wall, but blankets can be easily cut to length. Split the insulation where necessary to fit around your wiring or in narrow stud cavities. Size the pieces slightly long to give a tight fit. Choose insulation with attached vapor barriers except in very cold climates, where a continuous barrier should be applied over studs following insulation. The barrier should always face the side that's warm in winter. Hold back the insulation and barriers 3" from heat vents, electric heaters, recessed lights, and other heat-producing equipment. Stuff insulation scraps into any cracks and small spaces between the rough framing and windows and door jambs, and behind the electrical conduit, outlet and switch boxes, and other obstructions. Staple the barrier flanges to studs *(left)* and tuck in the loose ends. Never force too much insulation into a space, since there must be sufficient loft, or thickness, for it to be effective.

Insulating the attic

TOOLKIT
• Tape measure
• Utility knife
• Hand stapler

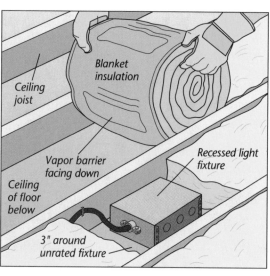

Ceiling joist

Blanket insulation

Vapor barrier facing down

Ceiling of floor below

Recessed light fixture

3" around unrated fixture

Installing insulation between joints
Insulate unfinished garage attics between the ceiling joists only. Place boards over the joists as makeshift flooring. Lay insulating blankets or batts with the attached vapor barrier down. If you're installing a separate vapor barrier, fasten it first to the sides of the joists. Extend the insulation over the top plates but don't block the eave vents. Leave 3" around any unrated heat producing fixtures *(left)*, and around vents and flues. Insulation can be laid over fixtures rated I.C. (insulated ceiling rating). Slit the batts to fit around wiring. For a finished attic, insulate between rafters, collar beams, short "knee wall" studs, and gable studs instead of ceiling joists. Face the vapor barrier in, toward the attic. Staple batts or blankets directly to the edges of rafters and studs.

ENCLOSING CEILING & WALLS

Although you may not be planning to make the interior of your garage or shed the most beautiful room on your property, if you want to finish interior walls and ceilings, you can install gypsum wallboard and finish it with your favorite color of paint.

Cutting and installing wallboard is straightforward, but the weight of the full panels can be awkward to work with—the panels are easily damaged if knocked or dropped. It's best to have a helper lend a hand, especially for the ceiling work.

Once the wallboard is cut and secured in place, it needs to be taped and finished. Concealing the joints between panels and in the corners requires patience and care. Buy precreased wallboard tape and pre-mixed joint compound. Textured compounds applied later will hide a less-than-perfect taping job, and any cracks between panels due to shifting will be less apparent. Ask your dealer for recommendations. The techniques shown below and on the following pages will help the work go smoothly.

Installing gypsum wallboard

TOOLKIT
- Straightedge or chalk line
- Utility knife
- Tape measure
- Wallboard or compass saw
- Perforated rasp (optional)
- Screw gun or bell-faced hammer

1 Cutting wallboard

To make a straight cut, first mark the cutting line on the front paper layer with a pencil and straightedge, or snap a chalk line. Cut through the front paper with a utility knife. Then turn the wallboard over and break the gypsum core by bending it toward the back. Finally, cut the back paper along the crease. When fitting wallboard around obstructions such as doorways, windows, or outlets, measure from the edge of an adjacent panel or reference point and up from the floor to the obstruction. For small cuts such as outlets, cut the opening about $1/8$" to $3/16$" bigger than needed. Transfer the measurements to a new panel and make the necessary cuts with a wallboard or compass saw. If the fit is tight, trim the board with a perforated rasp.

2 Supporting ceiling panels

When installing wallboard on the ceiling, the panels need to be supported when you're fastening them. It's usually easier to have a helper to do this. First, position a pair of step ladders, laying a few planks across them to serve as a short scaffold. Then, both you and your helper should hold your respective ends of the panel in place, using your heads. Carefully, begin to put the fasteners in, starting at the center of each panel. Then place the next few fasteners gradually closer to the ends of the panel, so the weight placed on your heads is decreased. Continue adding fasteners until the gypsum wallboard is firmly in place.

3 Installing the ceiling panels

When installing wallboard panels to both the ceiling and walls, apply the ceiling panels first, as shown at left. The edges of the ceiling panels will eventually be supported by the wall panels. Choose $1/2$"- or $5/8$"-thick panels, and fasten them perpendicular to the joists with annular ring nails, drywall screws, or a combination of nails and construction adhesive. Using screws installed with a screw gun is the easiest and fastest method. (Screw guns can be rented at tool rental stores.) Screw spacings are governed by local codes, but typical spacing is every 7" along the ends of panels and at intermediate joists (called "in the field"). Nails should be spaced at least $3/8$" in from the edges around the perimeter.

ASK A PRO

HOW DO I HOLD UP WALLBOARD?

If you don't have a helper to hold one end of the wallboard, you can construct one or two T-braces, as shown at right. The braces should extend from the floor to the ceiling joists; when the panel is positioned, the extra height will help wedge the brace in place.

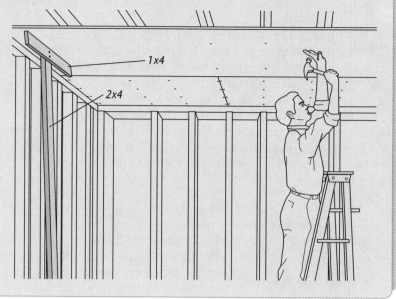

1x4

2x4

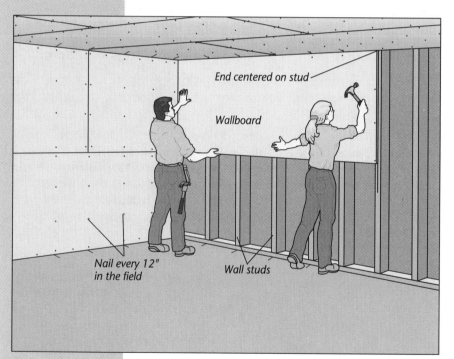

End centered on stud

Wallboard

Nail every 12" in the field

Wall studs

4 Installing the wall panels

Wallboard panels may be positioned either vertically or horizontally—that is, with the long edges either parallel or perpendicular to wall studs. Most professionals prefer the latter method *(left)*, because it helps bridge irregularities between studs, results in a stronger wall, and is easier to finish. Before installing the panels, mark all the stud locations on the floor and ceiling. Starting from one corner, lay the first panel tight against the ceiling. (If you choose the horizontal method, the panel ends may be either centered over studs or "floated" and tied together with backing blocks.) Make sure to stagger the end joints in the bottom row so they don't line up with the joints in the top row.

5 Fastening the panels

Wall panels can be secured in place with the same sort of fasteners used for the ceiling panels. Fastener spacings for wall panels are also subject to local building codes, but typical screw or nail spacing is every 8" along the panel edges and ends, and along the intermediate supports ("in the field"). Fasteners must be at least 3/8" in from the edges.

Use a bell-faced hammer, since your goal is to dimple the wallboard surface without puncturing the paper. If you do puncture it or miss a stud, pull out the nail and install another one.

It's usually simplest to first tack a row of panels in place with a few nails through each; later you can snap chalk lines to mark the studs, and then finish the nailing pattern.

TOOLKIT
- 6" and 10" taping knives
- Corner taping tool
- Putty knife (optional)

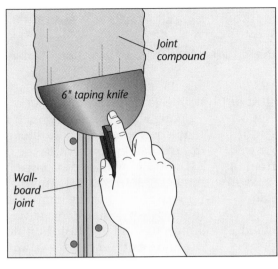

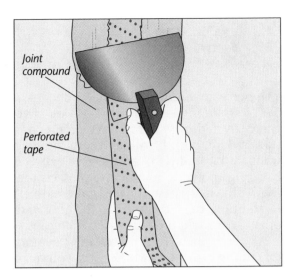

1 Taping joints between panels

Apply a smooth layer of joint compound over the joint with a 6" taping knife *(above, left)*. Before the compound dries, embed wallboard tape into it with the knife *(above, right)* and then apply another thin coat of compound over the tape, smoothing it gently with the knife. Use only enough compound to fill the joint and cover the tape evenly. Also, apply a thin coat of compound to any punctures in the panels, planning to add successive coats to level these surfaces even with the finished wallboard.

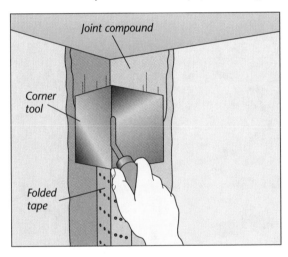

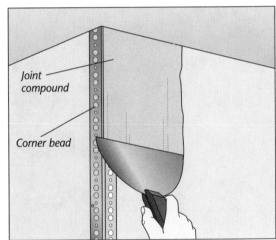

2 Taping the inside corners

Apply a smooth layer of compound to the wallboard on each side of the corner. Tear a piece of tape to length, fold it in half vertically, then press it into the corner with a corner taping tool or putty knife *(above)*. Then apply a thin layer of compound over the tape and smooth it out.

3 Finishing outside corners

Cover exterior corners with a protective metal corner bead cut to length and nailed through its perforations every 12". There's no need to tape (although it will reduce the chances of cracking); simply run your knife down the sharp metal edge to fill the spaces with compound *(above)*.

4 Applying successive coats

When all the joints and corners are taped, use smooth, even strokes with the 6" knife to cover the nail dimples in the field with a coat of the joint compound. When it has dried (it will look white, not gray), use a 10" knife to apply a second coat, feathering out edges past each side of the joint *(left)*. Let dry. Then sand and apply a final coat, using the 10" or an even wider finishing trowel to smooth out and feather the edges. After the final coat dries, sand with fine sandpaper to remove minor imperfections.

TRIM

Once you have installed the wallboard *(page 93)*, you can further improve the look of your shed or garage by adding wood trim. Contoured moldings or standard lumber trim along the bottom edge of your wallboard not only covers the gaps between your wall covering and your floor, it also protects the bottom of the wallboard. (For a nonwood alternative, see below.) In addition, the edges of both the door and window openings should have casing to hide gaps.

A miter box and backsaw are most commonly used for cutting trim. With a miter box, you can cut the pre- cise 45° and 90° angles necessary for most joints. If you're going to be doing a lot of cutting, or if you're working with unusual angles, it may be worthwhile to rent a power miter saw. Contoured moldings may re- quire coped joints at the inside corners, as shown below.

Door trim may be contoured molding or standard lumber. If you choose lumber, butt the joints at the top; for molding, miter the joints. Most windows require interior trim around the opening, which generally con- sists of top and side casings, a stool on top of the finish sill, and a bottom casing—or apron—below the stool.

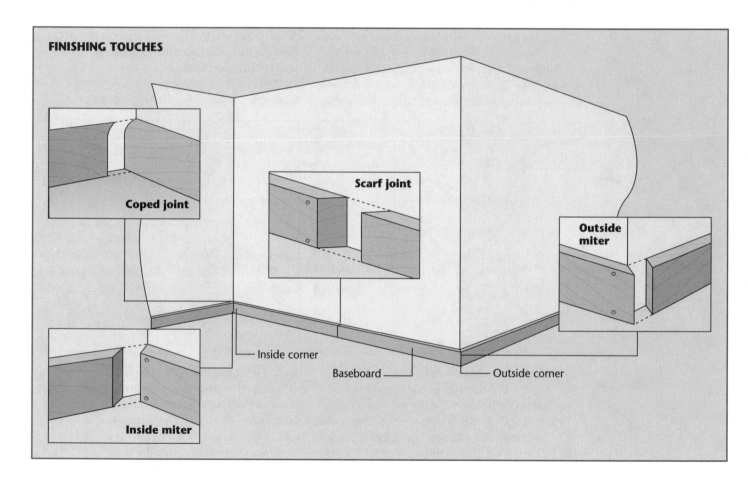

FINISHING TOUCHES

Coped joint

Scarf joint

Outside miter

Inside miter

Inside corner

Baseboard

Outside corner

 ASK A PRO

DO I HAVE TO USE WOOD TRIM?

As an alternative to traditional wood trim, use flexible vinyl or rubber cove base (also called wall base) to cover the gap between the bottom of the wallboard and the floor. Cove base comes in standard 4' lengths and is fastened to the wallboard with special adhesives for vertical surfaces. The lower edge rests on the floor, but isn't fastened to it.

Spread the adhesive with a notched trowel, and allow it to set as directed. Starting at an inside corner, press the base firmly in place until it holds. At outside corners, stretch it around the corner; at inside corners, cut it to fit, mitering the ends with a utility knife. Or, score the back of the mate- rial and bend it to form an inside corner without joints.

Cutting molding and coping a joint

TOOLKIT
- Backsaw and miter box
- Coping saw
- Combination square

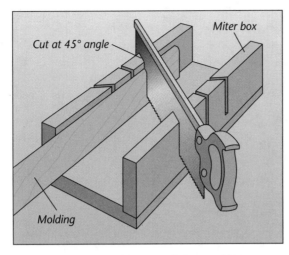

Cut at 45° angle / Miter box / Molding

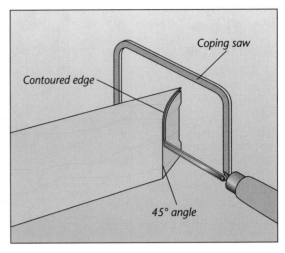

Coping saw / Contoured edge / 45° angle

Cutting and attaching straight moldings
Wood moldings should be installed with a slight gap between the floor and the molding; nail them to wall studs. Where two pieces join along a wall, miter the ends *(above)* to create a scarf joint. Nail through the joint to secure the pieces. At the outside corners, cut matching miters in each piece.

Coping a joint
Contoured moldings will require a coped joint at the inside corners for a smooth fit. To form a coped joint, cut the first piece of the molding square and butt it into the corner. Then cut the end of the second piece back at a 45° angle. Next, using a coping saw, follow the curvature of the molding's front edge while reinstating the 90° angle *(above)*. With a little practice, you can make the contoured end smoothly match the contours of the first piece.

Installing door casing

TOOLKIT
- Tape measure
- Backsaw and miter box
- Claw hammer
- Nailset
- Carpenter's level
- Combination square

1 ▶ Installing the side casing
Before installing the casing, pencil a "reveal" or setback line 1/4" in from the inside of each jamb. Align each of the side casings with this line and mark them where they intersect the top reveal line. Miter the ends from these points. (With flat lumber, you could choose to cut the corners square.) Tack the side casings in place while you install the top casing. Use 1 1/2" or 2" finishing nails to attach casing to the jamb, and 2 1/2" nails along the rough framing. Space nails every 16" *(right)*.

2 Installing the top casing
Measure between the tops of the side casings for the top casing, and miter the ends at 45°. If the door jambs are level and plumb, all should join snugly. If not, you'll have to adjust the angles of the top cuts to fit the side casings exactly. Nail all the casings in place; use 1 1/2" or 2" finishing nails to attach casing to the jamb, and 2 1/2" nails along the rough framing. Space nails every 16".

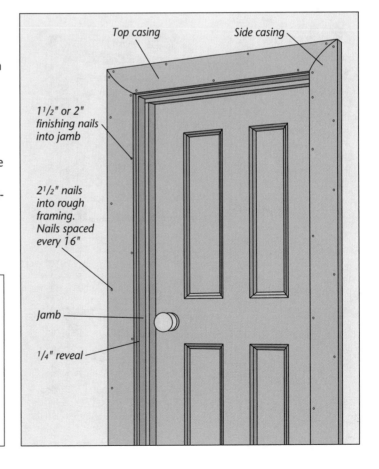

Top casing / Side casing

1 1/2" or 2" finishing nails into jamb

2 1/2" nails into rough framing. Nails spaced every 16"

Jamb

1/4" reveal

Installing window casing

TOOLKIT
- Tape measure
- Circular saw
- Combination square
- Claw hammer
- Nailset
- Backsaw and miter box (optional)

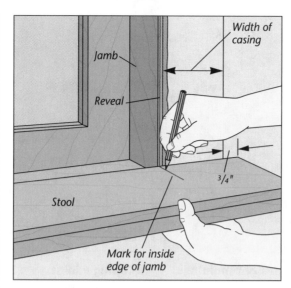

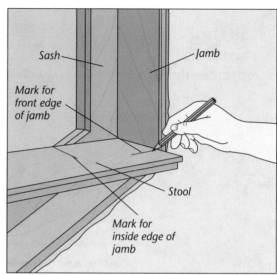

1 Installing the stool
Begin by penciling a $1/8$" or $1/4$" reveal just inside the side and top jambs; then measure the width of your casing. Add $3/4$" to the casing's width, double this figure and add the width of the window; this is the length you should cut the stool. Use either a flat piece of lumber or a preformed rabbeted or flat stool to meet the finish sill.

Center the stool over the opening and mark the center point on the stool and opening. Mark the inside edge of each side jamb on the stool's back edge (*above, left*). Place one end of the stool against a jamb, (the back edge flush with the window's sash) and mark the front edge of the jamb on the stool (*above, right*). Repeat this process for the other end. Using a combination square, extend each set of marks until they intersect; then notch the stool along the lines. Set the stool in place and fasten it to the finish sill with 2" finishing nails.

2 Installing the side and top casings
Square off one end of a piece of casing, and set that end on the stool, aligning the inside edge with the reveal. Mark the inside edge of the casing where the head jamb's reveal crosses it. Use a backsaw and miter box to cut the end at a 45° miter. Or, for flat lumber, you may prefer to cut the end square. Line up the inside edge of the casing with the reveal lines, and tack it so it stays in place while you fit the top casing. Repeat this process for the casing on the opposite side.

Measure the longest distance between the side casings, cut the casing to this length, then miter the ends at 45°. Align the three pieces, making adjustments if necessary before attaching them permanently. Nail the casings to the jamb with $1^1/2$" or 2" finishing nails, and to the rough framing with $2^1/2$" finishing nails.

3 Adding the apron
For the apron, cut a piece of molding the same length as the distance between the outside edges of the side casings. Center the apron under the stool, lining up its edges precisely with the casings' outside edges. Then attach it to the rough framing with 2" finishing nails.

BASIC STAIRWAYS

It's quite possible that your new garage will be a one-level structure, just large enough to park your car and store some garden equipment. But if you choose to have a two-level space, you'll need to build some stairs.

The type of stairway described here is "rough" (suitable in appearance for garage applications). These stairs are easier to build than they look, provided you follow certain basic rules, measure carefully, and plan each detail before you begin construction. Should you need to frame a new opening, or well, in the ceiling for your stairway, see the tip on page 100 for details.

Of course, there are more elaborate staircases than the one shown: these often involve decorative woodwork or changes in direction and elevation that require considerable skill in planning and execution. Although such stairs go beyond the scope of the basic information provided on these pages, the principles for building them are the same.

Three calculations are critical to your stairway plan: stairway angle, tread depth, and riser height. You also have to consider stair width, height of railings, and headroom. Check codes in your area for requirements.

Angle, treads, and risers: The angle of a stairway is a function of its riser/tread relationship. If the angle is too steep, the stairs will be a strain to climb. The ideal angle lies between 30° and 35°.

Normally the sum of the riser height and tread depth should be 17 to 18 inches. Ideal riser height is 7 inches (many building codes specify a maximum of 7½ inches).

Headroom, width, railings: To avoid having to duck every time you use the stairs, there must be adequate headroom. Most codes require a minimum headroom (from the front edge of the tread to any overhead obstruction) of 6½ feet. About 7½ feet is ideal, both for tall people and to avoid giving the stairway a closed-in feel.

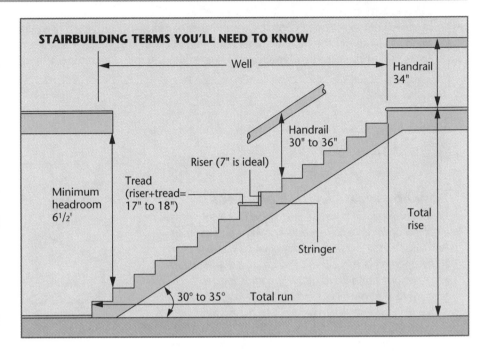

STAIRBUILDING TERMS YOU'LL NEED TO KNOW

Well • Handrail 34" • Handrail 30" to 36" • Riser (7" is ideal) • Minimum headroom 6½' • Tread (riser+tread= 17" to 18") • Stringer • Total rise • 30° to 35° • Total run

The width of the stair is less important and will be dictated largely by available space, but it should allow two people to pass. Building codes usually specify a 30-inch minimum; a width of 36 to 42 inches is preferable.

Handrailings 30 to 36 inches high (measured from the top of the front of the tread to the top of the railing) are comfortable for a person of average height; 34 inches is a good height above floors and landings. Many codes allow a maximum space of 4 inches between rails (6 inches is acceptable for the triangle below the bottom rail).

Materials: Because it provides the greatest strength, the best stringer design is the single-piece stringer with "sawtooth" cutouts for the steps. Use knot-free 2x12 lumber long enough to reach from the top landing to the floor at the correct angle, with one foot extra at each end.

For risers, select a knot-free grade of lumber not less than one inch thick (nominal dimension). It's common to use 2-inch nominal thickness boards for treads. You may want to purchase bullnosed treads and cut them to length.

Figuring your layout

TOOLKIT
• Tape measure
• Calculator

1 Calculating risers and treads

To determine the number of steps you'll need, measure the vertical distance—in inches—from floor to floor, and divide that measurement by 7", the ideal riser height. If the calculation is not a whole number, drop the decimal and divide the remainder into the vertical distance. The result will give you the exact measurement for each of your risers. For example, a total rise of 89"÷7"=12.7 steps. By dividing 89" by 12, you'll arrive at a riser height of 7.4".

Now take the exact riser height and subtract it from the ideal sum for both risers and treads—17½"—to find the exact depth of each tread. For safety, they must not measure less than 10".

2 Making the plan fit

Determine the total run (horizontal distance between top and bottom risers) to see if your plan will fit the space. Multiply your exact tread depth by the number of risers—minus one—to get the total run. If this run won't fit the space, adjust the riser/tread relationship, increasing the rise and decreasing the run—or vice versa—until you achieve a total run that will work. If you increase or decrease the height of each riser, you'll have to add or drop a step and recalculate. If a straight run proves too long, you may have to go to a return (180° change in direction) or L (90°) design.

ASK A PRO

HOW DO I FRAME A FLOOR OPENING?

When installing stairs, you'll need to plan for a floor opening. Floor openings require special framing—add trimmers, headers, and tail joists around any opening you're planning. If the opening is more than 4' wide, use double headers. Use joist hangers to attach headers longer than 6' to the trimmers, and tail joists longer than 12' to the headers. When assembling the framing, temporarily omit the full-length joist on each side to allow yourself nailing room. Install the initial trimmer joist on each side of the opening. Next, attach the first headers with three 3¹/₂" nails on each end. Cut the tail joists to length and nail them with 3¹/₂" nails too. Now add the second headers inside the first, nailing them through the trimmers as before, and face-nail them to the first headers. Finally, double the trimmers, nailing them together along their length and at the bottom edges with 3¹/₂" nails.

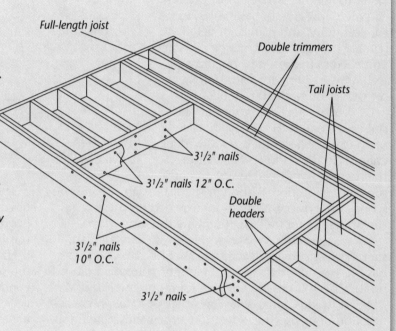

Full-length joist

Double trimmers

Tail joists

3¹/₂" nails

3¹/₂" nails 12" O.C.

Double headers

3¹/₂" nails 10" O.C.

3¹/₂" nails

Building the stairway

TOOLKIT
- Tape measure
- Carpenter's square
- Square gauges (optional)
- Circular saw
- Handsaw
- Claw hammer
- Wrench

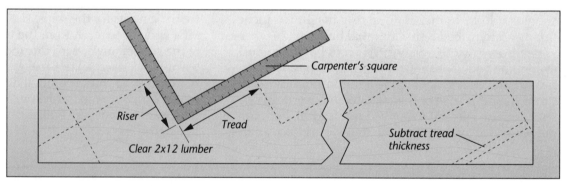

Carpenter's square

Riser

Tread

Clear 2x12 lumber

Subtract tread thickness

1 Laying out a sawtooth stringer

First, mark the height of the risers on the tongue of a carpenter's square; then mark the depth of the treads on the body. Alternately, you can use square gauges. Line up the marks with the top edge of the 2x12 stringer and trace the outline of the risers and treads onto it *(above)*. Cut out the notches, finishing with a handsaw.

Because the tread thickness will add to the first step height, measure the exact thickness of a tread and cut this amount off the bottom of the stringer. Check the alignment, then use this stringer as a pattern to mark the second one. If your stairway is 36" or wider, space a third stringer between the end stringers.

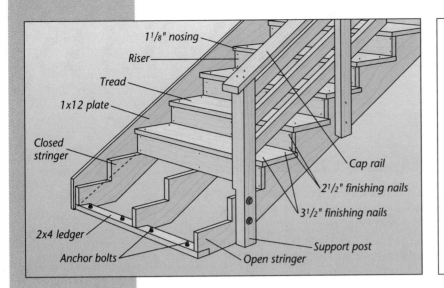

- 1⅛" nosing
- Riser
- Tread
- 1x12 plate
- Closed stringer
- 2x4 ledger
- Anchor bolts
- Cap rail
- 2½" finishing nails
- 3½" finishing nails
- Support post
- Open stringer

2 Nailing the stringer

Generally, nailing the top of the stringer to the rough opening's trimmers or headers is sufficient. However, you can increase strength by adding an extra header board, a plywood ledger, or metal joist hangers. At the bottom, cut notches in the stringers for a 2x4 ledger *(left)*. (Fasten the ledger to the floor with anchor bolts.)

If one or both of the end stringers will be "closed"—that is, attached to an adjacent wall—first nail an additional 1x12 plate to the wall studs: this acts both as trim and as a nailing surface for the main stair stringer.

3 Cutting and nailing the risers and treads

When measuring and cutting risers and treads, remember that the bottom edge of the riser overlaps the back of the tread, and the forward edge of the tread overlaps the riser below it. Giving each tread a 1⅛" nosing, or projection beyond the front of a riser, lends a more finished appearance.

Nail risers to the stringers, using 2½" nails. Then nail treads to the stringers with 3½" nails. Fasten the bottom edges of risers to the backs of treads with 2½" nails. Gluing treads and risers to the stringer as you nail them will help minimize squeaking.

4 Adding railings

Whether you use a simple length of 2x4 or purchase finished decorative railing, fasten the handrail securely to an inside wall with commercial brackets screwed to every third wall stud. For the open sides of your stairways, begin with sturdy posts not less than 2" square; bolt them directly to the stringer. Cap rails for outdoor and rough stairs are usually 2x4s or 2x6s nailed to each supporting post.

INSTALLING A PLYWOOD FLOOR IN A GARAGE ATTIC OR SHED

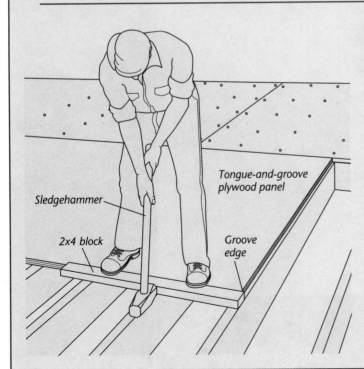

- Sledgehammer
- 2x4 block
- Tongue-and-groove plywood panel
- Groove edge

Tongue-and-groove plywood provides a serviceable floor for an attic storage area or a shed with a framed floor. Before you install the floor, you'll have to make sure that the ceiling joists that will support it are strong enough and properly spaced to support the weight *(page 53)*. It's best to plan for this when designing your garage. If you're unsure, consult your local building department for joist requirements.

Begin the first row by positioning the tongues to the outside. To fit the tongues of the second row into the grooves of the first, use a sledgehammer to hit a 2x4 wood block up and down the groove edge *(left)*, seating the tongue. When tacking the sheets, don't nail the groove edge or you'll have trouble fitting the next panel's tongue. For a sturdier fit, use both nails and an elastomeric construction adhesive. Gluing enables you to use fewer nails—space them 12 inches apart, both at panel ends and at intermediate supports. Use 2-inch ring-shank nails for panels up to ¾-inch thick, and 2½-inch nails for thicker panels.

GARAGE AND SHED PLANS

A new garage or shed can solve your storage problems, provide a protected area for your car, and add charm to your property. Among the plans on the following pages you're sure to find something to fit both your needs and your budget, whether you're looking for a simple shed to house your garden tools or an elaborate garage that extends your living space. And if you build it yourself, you'll have the added satisfaction of watching the structure take shape with each saw cut and swing of the hammer.

The following two pages provide information about how to order plans, including how to determine the number of copies you need, pricing, and an order form. Just choose the plan that's right for you from the selection beginning on page 105, follow the instructions to fill in the order form *(page 104)*, and mail it to us; you'll be well on your way to a new shed or garage.

A charming barn-style shed like this one may be just the added space you need: to use as a potting shed, or to store your gardening tools. Plans begin on page 105.

BEFORE YOU ORDER

Once you've chosen the one or two building plans that work best for you, you're ready to order blueprints. Before filling out the order form on the following page, note the information that follows.

HOW MANY BLUEPRINTS WILL YOU NEED?
Each plan package contains two sets of plans. This will allow you to study a design in detail. You may need more than one set for obtaining bids and permits, as well as some to use as reference at the building site.

For a major project such as a garage, figure you'll need at least one set each for yourself, your builder, the building department, and your lender. In addition, some subcontractors—foundation, plumber, electrician, and HVAC—may also need at least partial sets. If they do, ask them to return the sets when they're finished. The chart at right can help you calculate how many sets you're likely to need.

SERVICE AND PLAN DELIVERY
Service representatives are available to answer questions and assist you in placing your order. Every effort is made to process and ship orders within 48 hours.

RETURNS AND EXCHANGES
Each set of plans is specially printed and shipped to you in response to your specific order; consequently, requests for refunds cannot be honored. However, if the prints you order cannot be used, you may exchange them for another plan. For an exchange, you must return all sets of plans within 30 days. A nonrefundable service charge will be assessed for all exchanges; for more information, call our toll-free number (1-800-721-7027).

COMPLIANCE WITH LOCAL CODES AND REGULATIONS
Because of climatic, geographic, and political variations, building codes and regulations vary from one area to another. These plans are authorized for your use expressly conditioned on your obligation and agreement to comply strictly with all local codes, ordinances, regulations, and requirements, including permits and inspections at time of construction.

ARCHITECTURAL AND ENGINEERING SEALS
With increased concerns about energy costs and safety, many cities and states now require that an architect or engineer review and "seal" a plan for a large structure, such as a garage, prior to construction. To find out whether this is a regulation in your area, contact your local building department.

LICENSE AGREEMENT, COPY RESTRICTIONS, AND COPYRIGHT
When you purchase your plans, you are granted the right to use the documents to construct a single unit. All the plans in this publication are protected under the Federal Copyright Act, Title XVII of the United States Code and Chapter 37 of the Code of Federal Regulations. Each designer retains title and ownership of the original documents. The plans licensed to you cannot be used by or resold to any other person, copied, or reproduced by any means. If you require additional plans, you must order additional packets; each packet contains two complete sets of plans.

Complete the order form on the following page in three easy steps. Then mail in your order, or, for faster service, call our toll-free number (1-800-721-7027).

PLAN CHECKLIST

___ Set(s) for owner(s)

___ Builder usually requires at least three sets: one for legal documentation, one for inspections, and a minimum of one set for subcontractors.

___ Building department requires at least one set. Check with your local building department before ordering.

___ Lending institution usually requires at least one set.

___ **TOTAL SETS REQUIRED**

Remember: Each plan package contains two sets.

ORDERING PLANS

1. PLANS AND ACCESSORIES

Price Code	Description	Price
A	Small sheds and projects	$9.95
B	Garages	$12.95
C	Multi-use sheds and specialty buildings	$14.95
D	Specialty and multi-use garages	$24.95

Prices subject to change.
Each plan package contains two sets of plans.

2. SALES TAX AND SHIPPING

Determine your subtotal and add appropriate local state or provincial sales tax, plus shipping and handling charges from the chart below.

Shipping and handling charges

Type of Service*	Plan Package	2 Plan Packages	3 Plan Packages
U.S. Regular	$4.95	$7.95	$9.95
U.S. Express	$12.50	$15.50	$18.50
Canada Regular	$7.45	$9.95	$12.45
Canada Express	$18.00	$20.50	$23.00

* U.S. Regular (4-6 working days) U.S. Express (2-3 working days)
  Canada Regular (2-3 weeks) Canada Express (7-10 working days)

3. CUSTOMER INFORMATION

Choose the method of payment you prefer. Include a check, money order, or credit card information, complete the name and address portion, and mail the order form to:

Sunset/HomeStyles Plan Service
P.O. Box 50670
Minneapolis, MN 55405

FOR FASTER SERVICE, CALL
1-800-721-7027

ORDER FORM

Plan number _____   Price code _____

Number of packages _____ $ _____
                                (see chart at left)

Subtotal $ _____
Sales tax $ _____
Shipping and handling $ _____
GRAND TOTAL $ _____

Check/money order enclosed (in U.S. funds)
☐ VISA   ☐ MasterCard   ☐ AmEx   ☐ Discover

Credit card # _____ Exp. Date _____

Signature _____

Name _____

Address_____

City_____ State/Province_____

Country _____

Zip/Postal code_____

Daytime phone_____

Please check if you are a contractor. ☐

Mail form to: Sunset/HomeStyles Plan Service
              P.O. Box 50670
              Minneapolis, MN 55405

Or fax to: 612-338-1626

FOR FASTER SERVICE
CALL 1-800-721-7027

GABLE ROOF SHED

Ucando B2059
Price code A

Most roof configurations are variations on the basic gable roof. This design boasts a medium-high roof with a substantial pitch and a narrow span relative to length. A skylight and the circle top window above the Dutch door allow plenty of natural light.

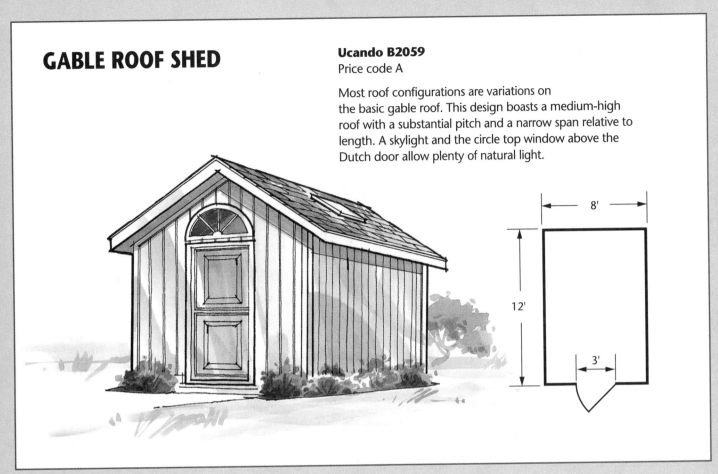

GABLE SHED WITH DOUBLE DOORS

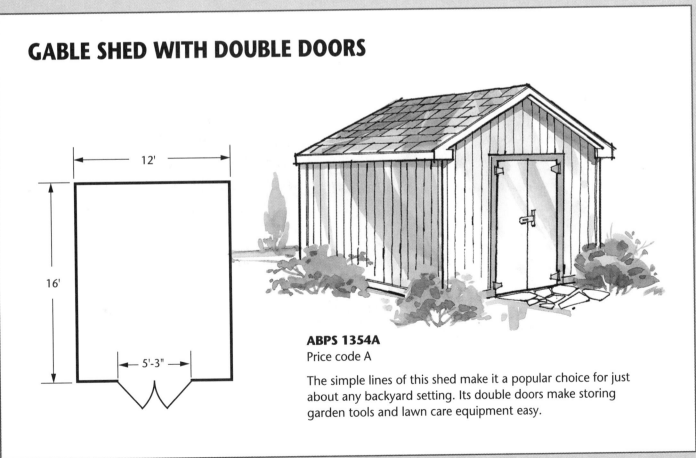

ABPS 1354A
Price code A

The simple lines of this shed make it a popular choice for just about any backyard setting. Its double doors make storing garden tools and lawn care equipment easy.

STORAGE BARN

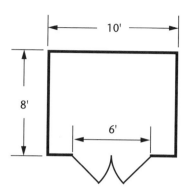

ABPS 1380
Price code A

The barn-style roof on this shed provides both rustic appeal and headroom for storing tall items such as ladders. Its double doors allow bulky items to be moved in and out without too much trouble.

GARDEN SHED WITH CUPOLA

Ucando B2009
Price code A

This traditional-looking shed gets its charm from the cedar plywood paneling, board-and-batten door, and cupola centered on the roof. It is ideal as a garden storage unit.

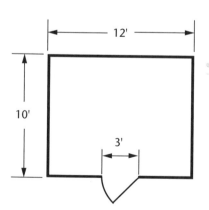

SALTBOX SHED

Ucando B2004

Price code A

The long rear slope of this shed's roof gives it a traditional saltbox look. With extra wide double doors and solid plywood flooring, this model is perfect for storing riding lawn mowers or patio furniture.

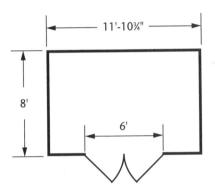

LITTLE BARN SHED

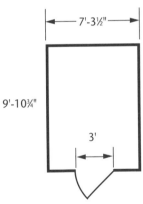

Ucando B2001

Price code A

This attractive addition to the backyard doesn't take up much space and can be used either for storage or as a playhouse for children.

BARN-STYLE SHED

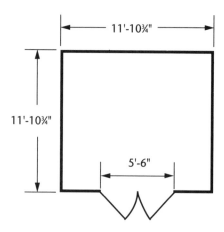

Ucando B2054
Price code A

The gambrel roof design and double doors on this shed make it ideal for storing almost anything from the backyard or garden. To maximize its floor-to-peak height of 9'4", you can lay longer items, such as lumber, across its exposed ceiling joists.

CLERESTORY SHED

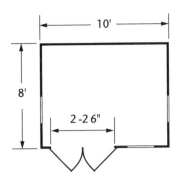

HPM 1403
Price code A

This shed is designed to provide plenty of natural light. It has clere-story windows at the roof, and windows in the doors and along the front and side walls. It's an ideal location for a small workshop or potting shed.

GREENHOUSE SHED

Ucando B2083
Price code A

Greenhouse windows installed in the long, south-facing slope on the roof of this shed provide good growing conditions for vegetables and flowers during colder months of the year.

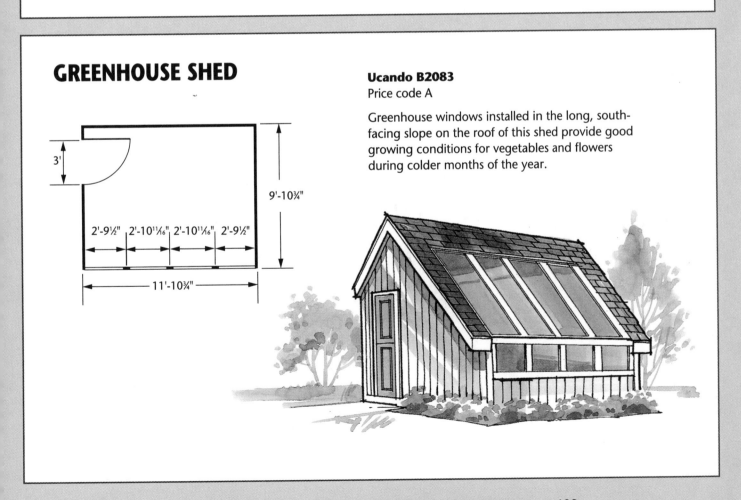

ATTRACTIVE CUPOLA

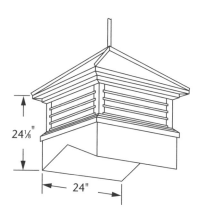

ABPS 1509
Price code A

This cupola is multifunctional. Apart from serving as a decorative element atop your shed roof, it also lets in air and light and serves as a base for a traditional weather vane. If your cupola is made of copper or any other metal, make sure it's grounded from lightning.

CHILDREN'S PLAYHOUSE

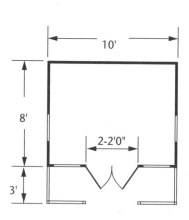

HPM 1400
Price code C

This cute little playhouse will give the kids a place of their own right out back. It has double doors, functional windows, and a front porch on which they can sit and sip lemonade.

DELUXE CABANA

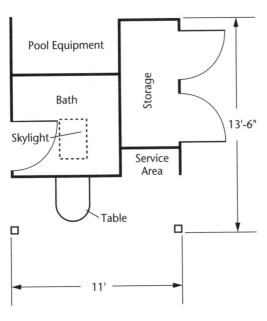

Pool Equipment

Storage

Bath

Skylight

Service Area

Table

13'-6"

11'

Ucando B2080

Price code A

Perfect for a home with a pool, this cabana has a convenient dressing room and a service area with a built-in table for late afternoon snacks. It can also be used for storing lawn furniture, and pool or sports equipment. Its unique roof design incorporates a skylight on one slope and a vent on the front face.

QUAINT WORKSHOP

HPM 1301
Price code C

This practical and attractive workshop/storage shed has double doors, a window planter box, and an entry ramp. A decorative touch at the peak of the roof adds to its charm. Inside, a workbench and cabinets offer the perfect setup for weekend projects.

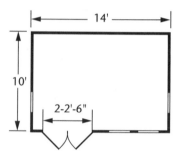

SIDE ENTRY WORKSHOP

HPM 1302
Price code C

This model has front doors and windows along what is traditionally the side of the unit. The high window flower boxes leave room for planting shrubs and bushes against the wall. The inside is roomy enough for storing tools and equipment, with enough extra space for a workshop.

WORKSHOP WITH PORCH

HPM 1300
Price code C

A combination workshop/storage shed, this model has front and side doors for both foot and equipment traffic, long windows to let in plenty of light, and a decorative porch for relaxing after working on a project. The workbench and cabinets are situated along the wall opposite the side doors.

SIMPLE CONVENIENCE SHED

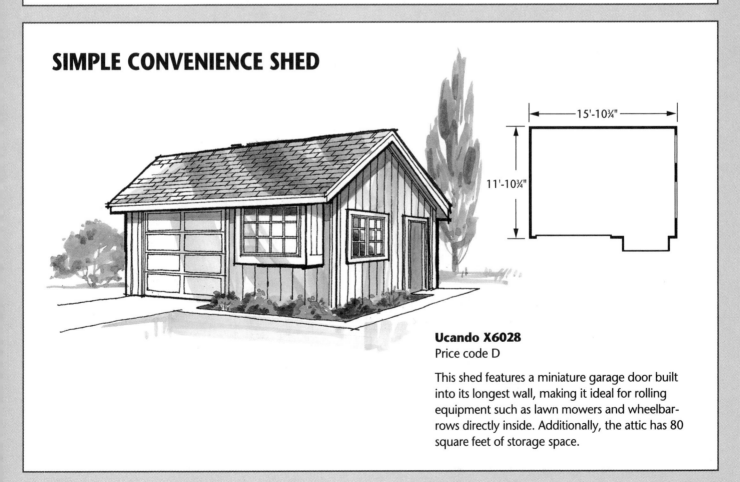

Ucando X6028
Price code D

This shed features a miniature garage door built into its longest wall, making it ideal for rolling equipment such as lawn mowers and wheelbarrows directly inside. Additionally, the attic has 80 square feet of storage space.

ONE-CAR GARAGE WITH STORAGE

Ucando P2015
Price code B

With the front door of this garage offset, there is room enough for parking a car and miscellaneous storage. You can add outdoor lights near both the car and service doors to make the garage more accessible at night.

CLASSIC TWO-CAR GARAGE

ABPS 3330
Price code B

The wide gable roof and double overhead door on this two-car garage give it its classic lines. A windowed door and window on the side wall provide natural light.

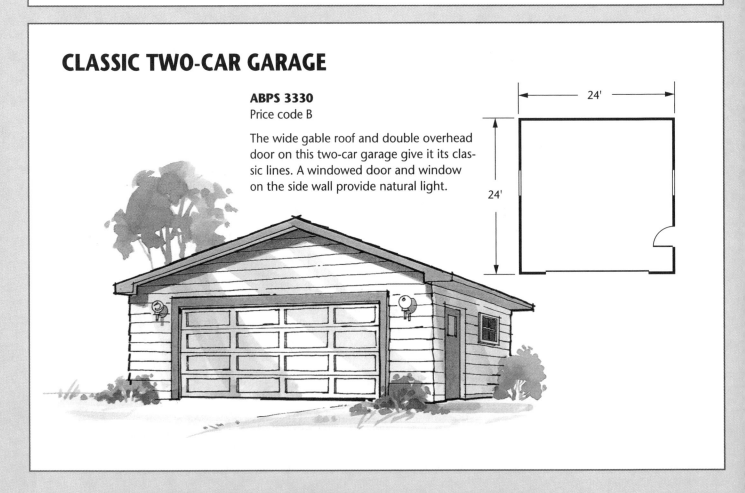

VICTORIAN-STYLE GARAGE

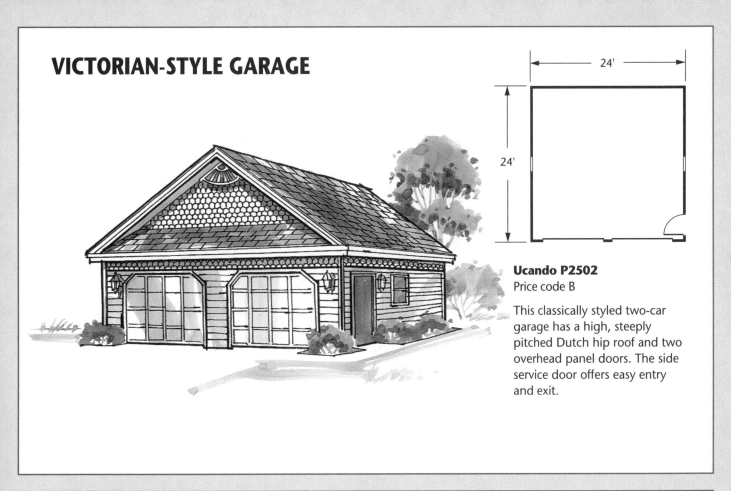

Ucando P2502
Price code B

This classically styled two-car garage has a high, steeply pitched Dutch hip roof and two overhead panel doors. The side service door offers easy entry and exit.

TWO-CAR GARAGE WITH STORAGE

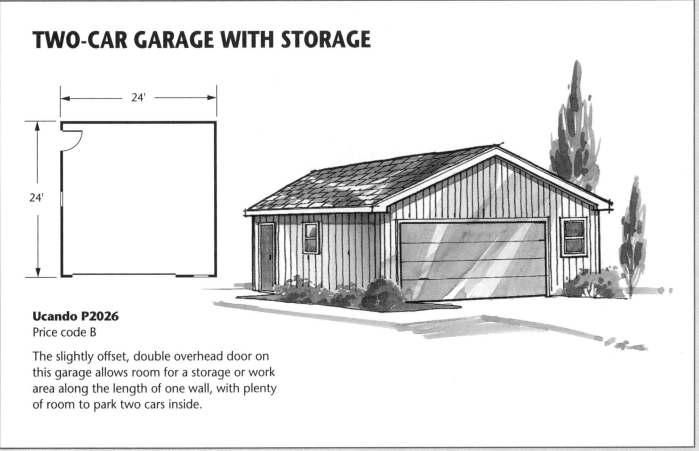

Ucando P2026
Price code B

The slightly offset, double overhead door on this garage allows room for a storage or work area along the length of one wall, with plenty of room to park two cars inside.

THREE-CAR GARAGE WITH LOFT

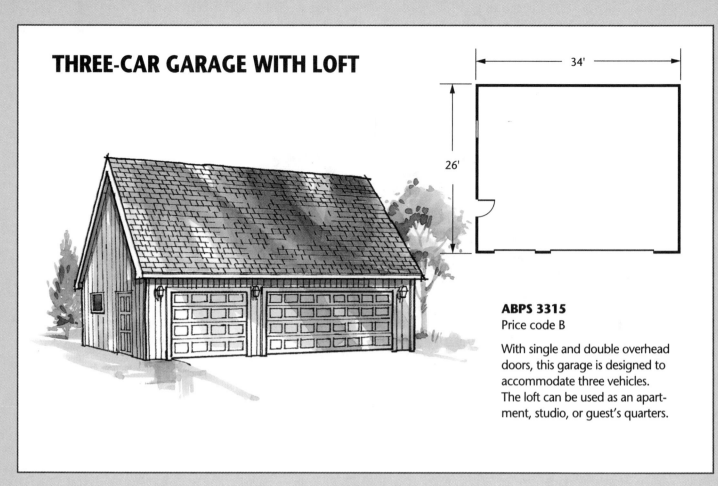

ABPS 3315
Price code B

With single and double overhead doors, this garage is designed to accommodate three vehicles. The loft can be used as an apartment, studio, or guest's quarters.

DOUBLE GARAGE WITH LOFT & DORMERS

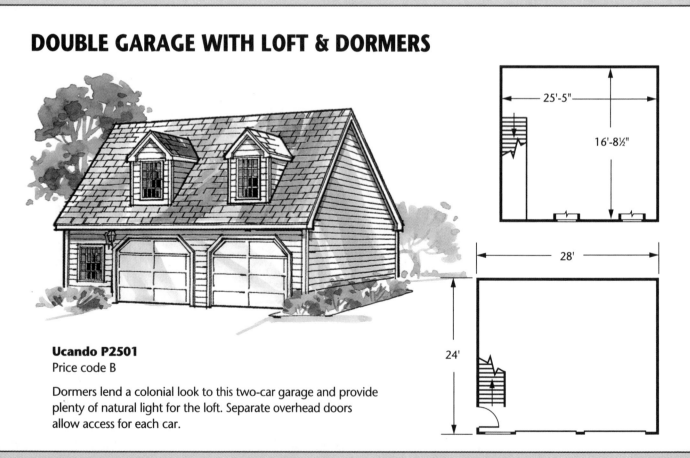

Ucando P2501
Price code B

Dormers lend a colonial look to this two-car garage and provide plenty of natural light for the loft. Separate overhead doors allow access for each car.

TWO-CAR GARAGE WITH WORK AREA

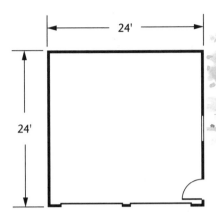

Ucando P2010
Price code B

This garage is designed to allow room for two cars with enough space at the back wall for a workbench or storage area. Its separate overhead panel doors offer an attractive facade. A side entrance allows easy access, while a window lets in light.

DOUBLE GARAGE WITH WORKSHOP AND LOFT

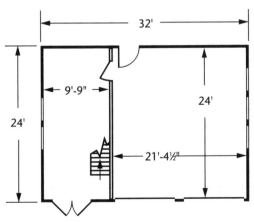

Ucando P2005
Price code B

Apart from two garage doors, this model has double entrance doors leading to storage space at the back, a workshop or hobby center in the corner, and access to a loft. The space above is useful as a studio, office, or guest room. Windows on the side wall provide light for both levels.

CREOLE GARAGE

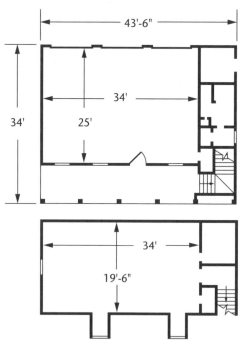

HPM V-cre-3
Price code D

This majestic garage offers more than a place to park cars and store lawn tools. It has a changing room/bathroom on the ground floor and a massive guest bedroom with connecting bathroom on the top floor. The covered porch and trimmed windows add to its rich appearance. Cars access the 25'x34' parking area—which also has plenty of room for storage—through the rear.

DOUBLE GARAGE WITH CARPORT AND GUEST QUARTERS

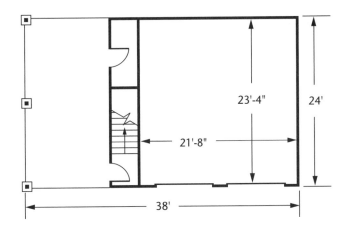

HPM A-369-1Q
Price code D

With this stylish garage, not only is there room for parking two cars inside, there's even an outdoor carport for a guest vehicle, or to be used for daytime parking. The interior houses a bathroom on both floors, plus a guest bedroom with a built-in kitchenette on the top level. A service door facing the carport offers easy entry to the lower level.

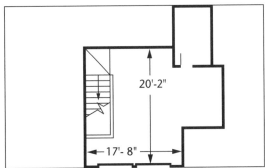

THREE-CAR GARAGE WITH LOFT

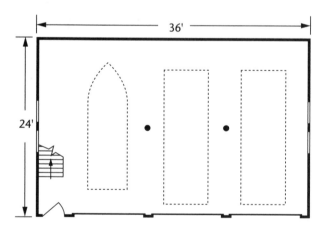

HPM N-673-GA
Price code D

This practical three-stalled garage with a long, sloping gable roof measures 36'x24', offering plenty of room to park a couple of cars and store a boat or a motorcycle, for example. A staircase leads to a loft that can be used as a studio, office, or simply a storage area. Double windows on the side wall provide natural light for both levels.

TWO-CAR GARAGE WITH APARTMENT

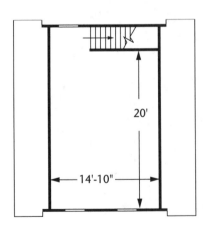 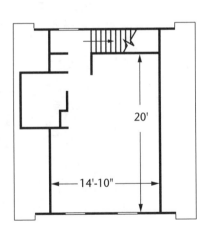 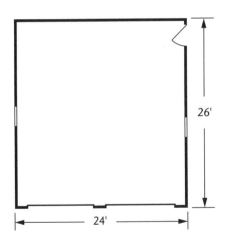

HPM N-674-GA
Price code D

This garage has a charming colonial look and is large enough to accommodate two vehicles on the main level and a spacious apartment, complete with kitchen and bathroom, above. A door at the rear provides a private entrance. Flower boxes under windows, and shutters on the sides, provide an attractive finishing touch.

TWO-CAR GARAGE WITH POTTING ROOM

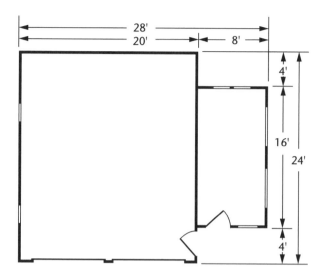

HPM 1001
Price code D

Two separate doors lead off the covered porch of this garage; one to a potting room, complete with shelves and a potting ledge, the other to a two-car parking area with a workbench at the rear. Windows on the two side walls and along the tops of the double garage doors allow plenty of natural light inside. Decorative motifs at each peak of the roof add a nice finishing touch.

TWO-CAR GARAGE WITH PORCH

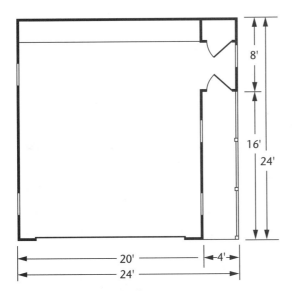

HPM 1000
Price code D

This unit's paneled overhead garage door with windows opens to reveal a two-car parking stall with space for a 42"-high workbench at the rear. Windows on the front and rear walls, as well as the dormers, make for a bright interior. A covered porch provides a cozy, shady place to relax outside.

TWO-CAR GARAGE WITH WORK AREA

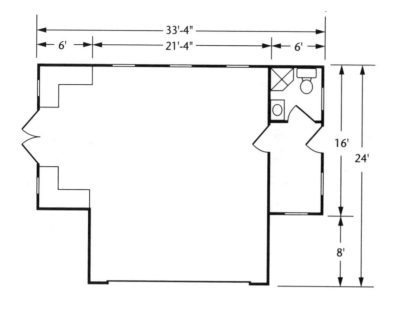

HPM 1005
Price code D

The substantial work area off to the side of the two-car parking space in this garage is an ideal location for doing repairs or working on week-end projects. The bathroom on the opposite side of the structure makes washing up easy. A path leading to a side entrance adds a domestic touch to the unit. Double hung windows on the main level, and a round-top window over the garage, let in plenty of light. Shutters add a finishing touch.

TWO-CAR GARAGE WITH STUDIO

HPM N-677-GA
Price code D

Two overhead panel doors provide access to parking in this garage, while an entry door opens to a staircase leading to a loft; a storage space is conveniently located behind the stairs. The studio apartment on the top level has a dining area, kitchen, and bathroom. Dormer windows keep the studio bright during the day.

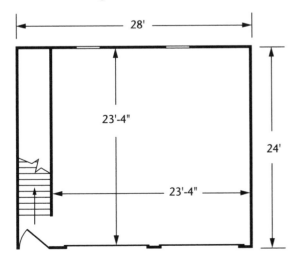

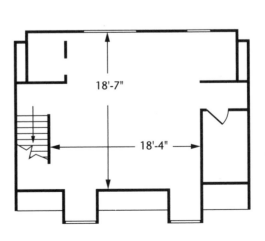

MULTIPURPOSE BARN

Ucando X6011
Price code D

This sturdy, no-nonsense barn, with a classic gambrel roof and wide, double sliding doors, is the perfect place to store just about anything. (An inside staircase leads to a second level.) The vertical plywood siding, 1"x4" trim, battens on the door, and asphalt shingles on the roof complete the overall rustic look. For an extra finishing touch, the siding is stained classic brown-red and the trim is painted white.

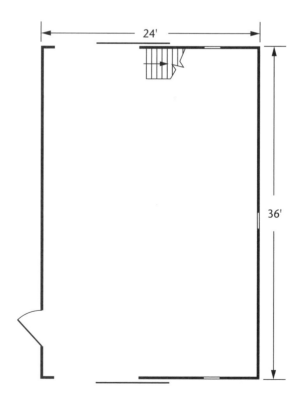

SHED & GARAGE GLOSSARY

Air-entraining agent
Added to concrete to make it more resistant to freeze-thaw damage. Also makes it more workable.

Anchor bolt
Used to fasten wood to concrete; the bolt, usually J-shaped, is set into freshly cast concrete with the threaded end projecting above the surface.

Batten
A thin strip of lumber used to seal vertical siding, or as a base for fastening some types of roofing.

Batterboards
Boards that support string used to lay out the foundation of a structure.

Bearing wall
A wall that supports joists at their ends or midspan, transferring weight to the girder, columns, or foundation wall below. All exterior walls, supporting the structure's weight, are bearing, as well as some interior walls.

Blocking
Pieces of wood installed between joists to give rigidity to the structure.

Cap
Fitting with a solid end used for closing off a pipe.

Cap rail
Part of a railing; horizontal member laid flat across the tops of the posts.

Curing
The process by which concrete/mortar hardens; works by keeping mortar moist for several days.

Dimension lumber
Lumber intended for structural framing and graded for strength. From 2" to 4" thick and at least 2" wide.

Drain tile
A masonry tube buried underground; carries ground water away from the structure.

Drip edge
Metal edging that fits on the edge of a roof to protect the fascia boards.

Expanding anchor bolt
A combined anchor and bolt used to fasten wood to masonry. The anchor bolt is tapped into a hole drilled in the masonry and a nut is tightened on the outside of the wood.

Face-nail
To drive a nail through one piece into another with the nail at right angles to the surface.

Fasteners
Any kind of hardware used to fasten one item to another; typically, nails, screws, and bolts.

Fire blocks
2-by lumber the same thickness as the studs, placed between the studs to prevent fire from spreading. Without it, this open space acts as a flue, drawing fire up from one level to higher ones.

Flashing
Material that seals a roof or wall at its vulnerable points, such as at valley and eaves.

Footing
The lowest part of a concrete foundation, which distributes the weight of the structure.

Framing connectors
A variety of metal connectors used to join wood to wood, or wood to concrete. Forms a stronger joint than nailing.

Frost heaves
Ground movement caused by freezing; can damage foundations.

Frost line
The maximum depth at which freezing can occur in a particular locale.

Galvanized
Fasteners that are covered with a hard coating of zinc that resists corrosion.

Ground fault circuit interrupter
A device that cuts a circuit in the event of a current leakage. It is either built into the circuit or installed in an individual receptacle. Abbreviated GFCI.

Header
A support piece framing an opening in a floor, wall, ceiling, or roof, at right angles to other framing members.

Hose bibb
Valve with an external threaded outlet for accepting a hose fitting.

Ice dams
Ice buildup at the eaves caused by thawing and refreezing, which can damage the structure.

Ice shield membrane
A rubber or plastic sheet that fits on the eaves to help prevent ice dams.

Joist
Horizontal wooden framing member, usually 2-by lumber, placed on edge, as in floor or ceiling joist.

Knee bracing
Short diagonal bracing fastened between a beam and the top of a post to add lateral stability.

Lag screw
A large screw with a square or hexagonal head; can be used instead of a bolt for heavy-duty fastening.

Ledger
A structural member attached to a house or other structure; supports the ends of joists.

Let-in bracing
Diagonal brace (wood or metal) that keeps the walls square; used as an alternative to sheathing for small buildings.

Live load
The weight put on a floor surface due to people, furniture, etc.

Mortise
A shaped cutout in a workpiece that commonly receives a tenon; also a recess for a hinge.

On center
The spacing between a series of objects as measured from the center of one to the center of the next. In plans, spacings are generally measured on center. Abbreviated O.C.

Plate
A horizontal framing member lying flat, usually made of 2-by lumber. Forms the top or bottom of a wall frame, as in the top plate or sole plate, respectively.

Plumb
Perfectly vertical. Also, to make vertical.

Rabbet
A 90° notch with two sides; on the edge or end of a piece of stock.

Rafter
An angled framing member that forms part of the sloping sides of a roof and supports the roof deck and roofing materials.

Rail
The horizontal element of a door structure.

Rim joist
A type of joist fastened across the ends of the other joists, and intended to keep the structure rigid.

Riser
The vertical part of a step.

Sheathing
The exterior skin of a structure under the siding; typically plywood.

Shim
A small piece of wood shingle, metal, or other rigid material used to adjust alignment, such as of a door or window frame, hinge, or strike plate.

Single-pole switch
A common type of light switch found in the home and small structures, these have two same-colored terminals, so either hot wire can connect to either terminal.

Soffit
The area below the eaves, where the roof overhangs the exterior walls.

Spade bit
A wide flat bit used to drill holes.

Span
The distance a member covers from the center of one supporting member to the center of the next.

Stile
The vertical member of a door structure.

Stringer
The diagonal part of a stairway supporting the risers and treads. Can be notched or cleated.

Stud
A vertical wood framing member; also referred to as a wall stud. Attached to sole plate below and top plate above.

Subfloor
Material such as plywood that forms a base for flooring materials. An underlayment may be applied between the subfloor and the flooring.

T-fitting
Or tee. T-shaped fitting with three openings.

Toenail
To drive a nail at an angle through one piece and into another.

Top cap
Ties walls together; fits on the top plate.

Tread
The part of a stair on which you walk.

Truss
An assembly of framing units that forms a rigid framework; typically for roofs.

Valley
The V-shaped meeting point of two roof planes.

Variance
An exception to zoning laws granted to a homeowner.

Wallboard, gypsum
A panel made with a core of gypsum rock, which covers interior walls and ceilings.

Window sash
The window component that holds the glass in place.

INDEX